A Facing History and Ourselves Publication

STORIES OF IDENTITY
Religion, Migration, and Belonging in a Changing World

With Afterword by Carola Suárez-Orozco

FACING
HISTORY
AND
OURSELVES

Facing History and Ourselves is an international educational and professional development organization whose mission is to engage students of diverse backgrounds in an examination of racism, prejudice, and antisemitism in order to promote the development of a more humane and informed citizenry. By studying the historical development of the Holocaust and other examples of genocide, students make the essential connection between history and the moral choices they confront in their own lives. For more information about Facing History and Ourselves, please visit our website at *www. facinghistory.org.*

Cover art photo: © Patrick Lux/DPA/epa/Corbis

To receive additional copies of this resource, please visit *www.facinghistory.org/publications.*

Printed in the United States of America
3 4 5 6 7 8 9 10
August 2010

ISBN-13: 978-0-9798440-3-4
ISBN-10: 0-9798440-3-7

FACING
HISTORY
AND
OURSELVES

Facing History and Ourselves Headquarters
16 Hurd Road
Brookline, MA 02445-6919

ABOUT FACING HISTORY AND OURSELVES

Facing History and Ourselves is a nonprofit educational organization whose mission is to engage students of diverse backgrounds in an examination of racism, prejudice, and antisemitism in order to promote a more humane and informed citizenry. As the name Facing History and Ourselves implies, the organization helps teachers and their students make the essential connections between history and the moral choices they confront in their own lives, and offers a framework and a vocabulary for analyzing the meaning and responsibility of citizenship and the tools to recognize bigotry and indifference in their own worlds. Through a rigorous examination of the failure of democracy in Germany during the 1920s and '30s and the steps leading to the Holocaust, along with other examples of hatred, collective violence, and genocide in the past century, Facing History and Ourselves provides educators with tools for teaching history and ethics, and for helping their students learn to combat prejudice with compassion, indifference with participation, myth and misinformation with knowledge.

Believing that no classroom exists in isolation, Facing History and Ourselves offers programs and materials to a broad audience of students, parents, teachers, civic leaders, and all of those who play a role in the education of young people. Through significant higher education partnerships, Facing History and Ourselves also reaches and impacts teachers before they enter their classrooms.

By studying the choices that led to critical episodes in history, students learn how issues of identity and membership, ethics and judgment have meaning today and in the future. Facing History and Ourselves' resource books provide a meticulously researched yet flexible structure for examining complex events and ideas. Educators can select appropriate readings and draw on additional resources available online or from our comprehensive lending library.

Our foundational resource book, *Facing History and Ourselves: Holocaust and Human Behavior*, embodies a sequence of study that begins with identity—first individual identity and then group and national identities, with their definitions of membership. From there the program examines the failure of democracy in Germany and the steps leading to the Holocaust—the most documented case of twentieth-century indifference, de-humanization, hatred, racism, antisemitism, and mass murder. It goes on to explore difficult questions of judgment, memory, and legacy, and the necessity for responsible participation to prevent injustice. Facing History and Ourselves then returns to the theme of civic participation to examine stories of individuals, groups, and nations who have worked to build just and inclusive communities and whose stories illuminate the courage, compassion, and political will that are needed to protect democracy today and in generations to come. Other examples in which civic dilemmas test democracy, such as the Armenian Genocide and the U.S. civil rights movement, expand and deepen the connection between history and the choices we face today and in the future.

Facing History and Ourselves has offices or resource centers in the United States, Canada, and the United Kingdom as well as in-depth partnerships in Rwanda, South Africa, and Northern Ireland. Facing History and Ourselves' outreach is global, with educators trained in more than 80 countries and delivery of our resources through a website accessed worldwide with online content delivery, a program for international fellows, and a set of NGO partnerships. By convening conferences of scholars, theologians, educators, and journalists, Facing History and Ourselves' materials are kept timely, relevant, and responsive to salient issues of global citizenship in the twenty-first century.

For more than 30 years, Facing History and Ourselves has challenged students and educators to connect the complexities of the past to the moral and ethical issues of today. They explore democratic values and consider what it means to exercise one's rights and responsibilities in the service of a more humane and compassionate world. They become aware that "little things are big"—seemingly minor decisions can have a major impact and change the course of history.

For more about Facing History and Ourselves, visit our website at *www.facinghistory.org.*

Acknowledgments

From its inception, *Stories of Identity* has been a collaborative effort. The staff, teachers, scholars, and friends of Facing History and Ourselves contributed ideas about the project's scope, themes, and source materials. We are deeply grateful to Mark Kingdon, who provided support and challenged us to create an educational resource that would help Facing History to reach new audiences and offer unique perspectives about the civic dilemmas of our age. Adam Strom headed this project and wrote much of the text, with the assistance of Jennifer Gray and Dan Eshet. Jennifer, who also served as the photo researcher, is responsible for the book's evocative images. Nicole Breaux, project manager, brought the myriad elements of this book into a cohesive and compelling whole. Josephine Roccuzzo was the copy editor, and Brown Publishing Network created the page design. Francesca Tramboulakis secured permissions for our use of copyrighted material. Marc Skvirsky's and Margot Stern Strom's leadership made this project possible; together they made numerous, thoughtful enhancements to the text. Marty Sleeper pored over the manuscript and provided valuable feedback and editorial suggestions. We are also grateful to Catherine O'Keefe and Robert Lavelle for their diligent efforts in turning a draft Word document into a published book.

Facing History and Ourselves would like to thank Carola Suárez-Orozco for her invaluable contribution to this collection. Her work, along with that of her husband, Marcelo, served as an inspiration for this project. Among the many people whose assistance and insight deserve special recognition, we would particularly like to thank Adrianne Billingham Bock, Alan Stoskopf, Amy Beckhusen, Anna Romer, Dennis Barr, Diane Moore, Dimitry Anselme, Doc Miller, Elisabeth Kanner, Jack Weinstein, Joy Lei, Juan Castellanos, Judy Wise, Karen Murphy, Steven Becton, Laura Tavares, Phyllis Goldstein, Riem Spielhaus, Zainab Al-Suwaij, Adam Brodsky, and Jeremy Nesoff.

Table of Contents

Preface

By Adam Strom, Director of Research and Development,
Facing History and Ourselves

"As new arrivals reshape the landscapes of public spaces, they change our perceptions of home and self; ultimately, each of these stories is about the impact of globalization on identity."

T he cries of some commentators notwithstanding, immigration is hardly a new phenomenon. People have migrated from place to place, resettling and making new lives for themselves, since before the creation of modern nation states. For the migrants, relocating meant finding a way to adapt to life in new lands. For the host society, migration often pushed the bounds of tolerance, forcing communities to consider how much difference they can tolerate and what rights, if any, they would extend to the newcomers. Facing History and Ourselves' resources, such as *Facing History and Ourselves: Holocaust and Human Behavior, Race and Membership in American History*, and *Becoming American: The Chinese Experience,* have highlighted a number of these stories. They reveal how myths about national and racial purity, along with stereotypes and fear, have influenced the choices made by host societies—individuals, groups, and nations—about whether and how immigrants should be accepted into the worlds they consider their own.

Since the end of the twentieth century, the convergence of migration and globalization has reshaped the public debate about differences. These already difficult dialogues have been complicated by terrorism and a resurgence of ethnic violence. Whereas once a single language, a single skin color, or a shared faith defined a community, the time has come for a new definition that acknowledges differences and finds common meaning and purpose in ideals and hopes that transcend history and genealogy. As new ideas, customs, and people make their way into older, more traditional communities, immigration raises dilemmas for migrants and nonmigrants alike. *Stories of Identity: Religion, Migration, and Belonging in a Changing World* focuses on a cross-section of individuals and societies, using memoirs, journal articles, interviews, and other primary sources to examine shifting cultural boundaries and the challenges of integration. For as new arrivals reshape the landscapes of public spaces, they also change our perceptions of home and self. Thus each of these stories is about the impact of globalization on identity.

▲ Brick Lane in the East End of London

Sociologist Manuel Castells has affirmed the modern need to investigate our very selves, explaining, "In a world of global flows of wealth, power, and images, the search for identity—collective or individual, ascribed or constructed—becomes the fundamental source of social meaning."[1] Glimpses of these "global flows" have underscored the questions about identity and belonging that begin every Facing History and Ourselves study and help to illuminate the challenges that young adults encounter. How can the world's teachers help students deal with the new, the unfamiliar, and the complex? How will students learn to take the perspective of another in order to understand whether the newly arrived and the long ensconced have to compromise their core values? What can educators do to promote tolerance, respect, and understanding?

The readings in this collection explore the dilemmas of integration in our globalized world. In the twentieth century, debates about integration often revolved around race, nationality, or social class. Increasingly, however, religion has become the important marker of identity in the discussions about attachment and membership. Religious identities mean different things to different people. For some it is a matter of faith. For others, religious attachments are cultural. Still others define themselves as secular, or without religious attachments.

Many of the narratives in this book involve Muslims in England and France and reflect similar stories playing out across Europe. Today Muslims are the largest and most visible religious minority in Europe. Sociologist Tariq Modood notes, "With an estimated 15 million Muslims in Western Europe today, about four percent of the population, they are larger than the combined populations of Finland, Denmark, and Ireland. For this, if no other reason, Muslims have become central to the merits and demerits of multiculturalism as a public policy in western Europe."[2] In fact, in almost every European country (the United Kingdom is a significant exception), most nonwhites are Muslim, and the struggles of Muslims can be seen as representing the challenges faced by other minority populations.[3] In the debates over Muslim integration, many Europeans are rethinking their own assumptions about the role of religion in public life and its historical relationship to national identity across the continent. French religious scholar Olivier Roy explains that "Islam is a mirror in which the West projects its own identity crisis."[4]

Associated Press/Alexandra Boulat

▲ Young Turkish women gather outside a store in the predominantly Turkish district of Kreuzberg in Berlin, Germany.

Added to these discussions about religious differences are the thorny questions of how to respond to terrorism and religious extremism that have arisen since the attacks in New York, Washington, London, and Madrid.

Yet, to talk about Muslims collectively can be misleading, since, like many other "groups," they are not a single, homogeneous entity. Followers of the Qur'an—like those who follow the Bible or the Torah—express their identities differently as individuals, families, and regional groups. The expectation of prosperity and security draws families from areas as diverse as India and Pakistan, Algeria and Morocco, the Persian Gulf and Turkey to settle in a single country, which adds to the complexity. The idea that being Muslim is a more important marker of identity than country of origin or status as a guest worker or former colonial subject is a recent phenomenon. As an antidote to the stereotypes about Muslims in the media, the readings in this collection emphasize the diversity of the Muslim community as well as some of the shared dilemmas its members face as they struggle to adapt to life in the West. Their particular stories allow us to explore more universal challenges of integration.

Although it once was possible to imagine our communities as distinct and autonomous, the flow of people, ideas, goods, and money leaves little doubt that no part of the world is untouched by the powerful forces of globalization. One of the most visible aspects of globalization is migration—from rural areas to cities, from one region or country to another, or from a familiar country to a quite foreign one. As people cross national borders, they carry with them their identities—their culture, religion, and values. Since the communities where migrants settle have their own identities, each community accommodates newcomers in its own way. The relationship between the newcomers and their host societies is shaped by the reach of what anthropologist Benedict Anderson calls "imagined communities." A century ago, common experiences reinforced by strong central governments made the state an important part of an individual's identity. Today, cellular phones, text messaging, the Internet, and the general speed of news and information encourage people to imagine different sorts of communities that have little to do with local or national boundaries.

Amin Maalouf, the author of *In the Name of Identity: Violence and the Need to Belong,* grew up in Lebanon and now lives in France. He believes that much of the world's violence arises from the way people negotiate issues of identity.

"In the age of globalization and of the ever-accelerating intermingling of elements in which we are all caught up, a new concept of identity is needed, and needed urgently. We cannot be satisfied with forcing billions of bewildered human beings to choose between excessive assertion of their identity and the loss of their identity altogether, between fundamentalism and disintegration."[5]

Forcing people to choose between one identity and another, between being French or Lebanese, American or Korean, exacerbates tensions and widens the divide between "us" and "them." Maalouf urges us to recognize the multiple identities we all hold—and he is not alone. Despite the pressure to choose a label, many young people have begun to identify themselves as mixed, bicultural, or transnational.

There is a paucity of written reflections on identity by members of what we might call the "host societies." At a recent forum on Muslims in the

New Yorker/Glen Le Lievre

"Actually, I prefer the term Arctic-American."

West, two Dutch politicians spoke. One of them, a Muslim woman whose family is from Morocco, commented on the evolution of her identity after September 11. The other, a Dutch man, struggled to describe his own identity. Dutch? Yes, like the previous speaker. Christian? Well, no: he's not very religious. What could he call himself? His playful reply: "How about a white guy?"[6] Identity, he reminded us, is as much a problem for members of host communities as for immigrants and their children. Still, white, mostly Christian Europeans like him, who share the nationality of their grandparents, rarely mull over their identities in print. Such modest reflections are drowned out by the media blare of far-right anti-immigrant or anti-Muslim politicians. From France's National Front and England's British National Party to the Austrian Freedom Party, these nativists are exerting an increasing influence over the immigration debate in Europe. Preferring to focus on the stories of ordinary people and not the politics, we have included a number of readings about communities balancing their historical identities with the demands of pluralism.

The readings in the first section of this book, "Frameworks," offer vocabulary and useful terminology for the materials that follow. Through stories and personal reflections, the readings in this section introduce ideas about people's response to difference as well as ways to think about models of integration. Other readings in this section provoke discussion on individual and national identities in our changing world.

The next set of readings, "Dilemmas of Integration," focuses on particular stories to highlight the social challenges faced both by newcomers and host societies. Several of these stories confront the delicate negotiations concerning the role of religion in personal and public life. For example, the reading on the experience of Jews in Britain provides a historical point of comparison for current debates. Until recently, Jews were the most prominent religious minority in the United States and Europe; for generations, their experiences defined the encounters and coexistence of religious minorities with Christians. Similarly, the reading "From Foreigners to Muslims" echoes the dilemmas of integration by exploring the creation of Muslim identity in contemporary Europe. These stories, while particular, serve as a reminder that group identities are dynamic—they are created from the inside and outside. Other stories in this section reflect the difficulties migrants and host societies face as they negotiate their changing communities.

The concluding section, "Identity and Belonging in a Globalized World," offers new ways of thinking about integration. The book ends with an afterword by cultural psychologist Carola Suárez-Orozco that summarizes her groundbreaking work on migration and identity development and adds another perspective to the stories and readings in this collection.

Facing History and Ourselves believes that schools, as public institutions, must foster ongoing dialogues about creating respectful pluralistic communities. In one of the stories from this collection, Eboo Patel, the founder of Interfaith Youth Core, describes his failure to respond vigorously to encounters with antisemitism. He found that when you lack the words, you can hardly describe a tradition—and when you can't describe it, you can hardly defend it.[7] Too often, rumor and misinformation fill the void. This book provides resources to begin constructive conversations. As educators preparing the next generation for life in a diverse and shrinking world, we have an obligation to fill this void with well-informed, thoughtful, and meaningful discourse.

[1] Manuel Castells, *The Rise of the Network Society*, 2nd ed. (Oxford: Blackwell, 2000), 3.

[2] Tariq Modood, *Multiculturalism: A Civic Idea* (Cambridge: Polity Press, 2007), 4.

[3] Ibid.

[4] Olivier Roy, *Secularism Confronts Islam* (New York Chichester, West Sussex: Cambridge University Press: 2007), xiii.

[5] Amin Maalouf, *In the Name of Identity: Violence and the Need to Belong* (New York: Arcade 2001), 35.

[6] "Muslim Identities, Western Identities: New Approaches and New Leaders for Conciliation" (conference, The International Center for Conciliation, Cambridge, MA, October 22, 2007).

[7] Eboo Patel, *Acts of Faith: The Story of an American Muslim, the Struggle for the Soul of a Generation* (Boston: Beacon Press, 2007), XVIII.

◇ ◇ ◇

Frameworks

◇ ◇ ◇

Understanding Strangers

"That same choice our ancestors faced thousands of years ago faces us today as well, with undiminished intensity—a choice as fundamental and categorical as it was back then. How should we act toward Others?"

▲ Two Muslim girls hold hands as they enter a religious festival with Sikhs at school in Britain.

Jim Watson/AFP/Getty Images

Journalist Ryszard Kapuscinski explains that an "encounter with the Other, with other people, has always been a universal and fundamental experience for our species." The question he asks is, Do those encounters lead to violence or to cooperation, to bridge building or to the building of walls?

Archaeologists tell us that the very earliest human groups were small family-tribes numbering 30 to 50 individuals. Had such a community been larger, it would have had trouble moving around quickly and efficiently. Had it been smaller, it would have found it harder to defend itself effectively and to fight for survival.

So here is our little family-tribe going along searching for nourishment when it suddenly comes across another family-tribe. What a significant movement in the history of the world, what

This reading contains excerpts from Ryszard Kapuscinski's, "Encountering the Other: The Challenge for the 21st Century," and Fatema Mernissi's, *Scheherazade Goes West: Different Cultures, Different Harems.*

a momentous discovery! The discovery that there are other people in the world! Until then, the members of these primal groups could live in the conviction, as they moved around in the company of 30 to 50 of their kinfolk, that they knew all the people in the world. Then it turned out that they didn't—that other similar beings, other people, also inhabited the world! But how to behave in the face of such a revelation? What to do? What decisions to make?

Should they throw themselves in fury on those other people? Or walk past dismissively and keep going? Or rather try to get to know and understand them?

That same choice our ancestors faced thousands of years ago faces us today as well, with undiminished intensity—a choice as fundamental and categorical as it was back then. How should we act toward Others? What kind of attitude should we have toward them? It might end up in a duel, a conflict, or a war. Every archive contains evidence of such events, which are also marked by countless battlefields and ruins scattered around the world.

But it might also be the case that, instead of attacking and fighting, this family-tribe that we are watching decides to fence itself off from others, to isolate and separate itself. This attitude leads, over time, to objects like the Great Wall of China, the towers and gates of Babylon, the Roman *limes* and the stone-walls of the Inca.

Fortunately, there is evidence of a different human experience scattered abundantly across our planet. These are the proofs of cooperation—the remains of marketplaces, of ports, of places where there were agoras and sanctuaries, of where the seats of old universities and academies are still visible, and of where there remain vestiges of such trade routes as the Silk Road, the Amber Route and the Trans-Saharan caravan route.

All of these were places where people met to exchange thoughts, ideas and merchandise, and where they traded and did business, concluded covenants and alliances, and discovered shared goals and values. "The Other" stopped being a synonym of foreignness and hostility, danger and mortal evil. People discovered within themselves a fragment of the Other, and they believed in this and lived confidently. People thus had three choices when they encountered the Other: They could choose war, they could build a wall around themselves, or they could enter into dialogue.[1]

Moroccan scholar Fatema Mernissi remembers the advice of her grandmother, Yasmina, who felt that each encounter with strangers was a chance to learn. An internationally known scholar, Mernissi now travels the world and tries to remember Yasmina's lessons.

▲ Author Fatema Mernissi (right) meets Prince Felipe of Spain.

If by chance you were to meet me at the Casablanca airport or on a boat sailing from Tangiers, you would think me self-confident, but I am not. Even now, at my age, I am frightened when crossing borders because I am afraid of failing to understand strangers. "To travel is the best way to learn and empower yourself," said Yasmina, my grandmother, who was illiterate and lived in a . . . traditional household with locked gates that women were not supposed to open. "You must focus on the strangers you meet and try to understand them. The more you understand a stranger and the greater is your knowledge of yourself, the more power you will have. . . ."

. . . [A]ccording to Yasmina's philosophy, which I later discovered she had adopted from the Sufis, the mystics of Islam, I needed to transform my feelings of shock toward the Western journalists [I encountered] into openness to learn from them. At first, I had great difficulty doing so and started wondering if perhaps, due to my age, I was losing my capacity to adapt to new situations. I felt terrified of becoming stiff and unable to digest the unexpected. . . .

To learn from travel, one must train oneself to capture messages. "You must cultivate *isti'dad*, the state of readiness," Yasmina used to whisper conspiratorially in my ear, so as to exclude those whom she regarded as unworthy of the Sufi tradition. "The most baggage carried by strangers is their difference. And if you focus on the divergent and the dissimilar, you get 'flashes.'"[2]

Connections

1. If we want to understand others better, is it more helpful to focus on similarities or differences? According to Kapuscinski, what are the three possible ways to respond to the Other?

2. How have you responded to individuals or groups who are different from you? Why? What factors influence the choices people make about how to respond to difference?

3. Kapuscinski writes about times when "'[t]he Other' stopped being a synonym of foreignness and hostility, danger and mortal evil" and people "discovered within themselves a fragment of the Other." What does Kapuscinski mean when he writes about discovering fragments of "the Other" in ourselves?

4. Fatema Mernissi's grandmother believed that "the more you understand a stranger . . . the more power you will have." What did she mean? Do you agree with her statement? What can you learn from people who have grown up with religions, cultures, and habits that are different from your own? What do you think are the "flashes" she referred to?

◇ ◇ ◇

¹ Ryszard Kapuscinski, "Encountering the Other: The Challenge for the 21st Century," *New Perspectives Quarterly*, vol. 22 #4 (Fall 2005) *http://www.digitalnpq.org/archive/2005_fall/02_ kapuscinski.html* (accessed November 8, 2007).

² Fatema Mernissi, *Scheherazade Goes West: Different Cultures, Different Harems* (New York: Washington Square Press, 2001), 1–4.

Three Parables for Integration

"How should societies integrate newcomers? How do newcomers develop a sense of belonging to the places where they have arrived?"

According to anthropologist Marcelo Suárez-Orozco "globalization defines our era." He defines globalization as the "movement of people, goods, or ideas among countries and regions." Essential to globalization is the impact of migration—from country to city and from nation to nation. Speaking to educators, Suárez-Orozco explained that there are 175 million immigrants and refugees worldwide. And those new migrants are changing the composition of the cities where they live. Orozco uses statistics to illustrate his point:

> Leicester, England, will be the first European city with [a] non-white majority. Frankfurt today is about 30% immigrant; Rotterdam is 45% immigrant. Amsterdam will by [the] year 2015 be 50% immigrant. Sweden has 1 million immigrants. China alone has over 150 million internal immigrants. . . . In the New York City schools the children of immigrants are half the total population . . . with over 190 nationalities represented.[1]

How should societies integrate newcomers? How do newcomers develop a sense of belonging to the places where they have arrived? These are the questions Chief Rabbi of the British Commonwealth, Jonathan Sacks, considers in his book *The Home We Build Together*. Sacks, a leader in the Jewish community and an advisor to politicians and policymakers, offers three different parables about the relationship between newcomers and their host societies as a way to provoke discussion about assimilation and integration.

This reading contains excerpts from Jonathan Sacks's, *The Home We Build Together*.

Mireya Leal shares a picnic lunch through the US-Mexico border fence with her husband Raymundo Orozco. ▶

In the first, a hundred strangers have been wandering around the countryside in search of a place to stay. Eventually they arrive at the gate of a large country house. The owner comes to the gate, sees the strangers and asks them who they are. They tell him their story. He gives them a warm smile. "How good to see you," he says. "As you can see, I have an enormous home. Far too big for me, actually. There are hundreds of empty rooms. Please feel free to stay here as long as you like. I look forward to your company. From now on consider yourself my guests."

A lovely story. But not entirely so for the strangers in the long run. They have a place to live, and yes, their host is exactly as he seemed at first, welcoming, hospitable. . . . However there is only one thing wrong as far as they are concerned. However generous their host, he remains the host and they are his guests. The place belongs to someone else. That is *society as a country house*.

The second: A hundred strangers in search of a home find themselves in the middle of a big city. They are there to find a hotel. It is large, comfortable, and has every amenity. The visitors have money enough to pay the hotel bills. They book their rooms, unpack, and stay.

The rules are simple. They are free to do what they like, so long as they don't disturb the other guests. Their relationship with the hotel is purely contractual. They pay money in return for certain services. . . .

The hotel offers the newcomers a freedom and equality they did not have in the first model. They are guests, but so is everyone else. There is only one problem. A hotel is where you stay, not where you belong. You feel no loyalty to a hotel. You don't put down roots there. It doesn't become part of your identity. . . . Yes, after a while you recognize your fellow guests. You bid them good morning. You discuss the weather and football. But it remains a place where everyone is, in the biblical phrase, "a stranger and sojourner." That is *society as a hotel*.

The third: A hundred strangers arrive at a town. They are met by the mayor, councilors and local residents. The mayor says: "Friends, we welcome you. It is good to have you among us. Sadly, as you can see, there is no country house where we might accommodate you. There is, though, something we can offer you.

"We have a patch of empty land: large enough to accommodate homes for all of you. We have bricks and materials. We have experts who can help you design your homes, and we will help you build them. . . . Let us do this together."

So it happens. Unlike the country house, the newcomers have to build their own long-term accommodation. Unlike the hotel, they do not merely pay. They invest their energies in what they build. . . . They helped build it.

Sacks explains that it won't always be easy.

The newcomers still occasionally seem strange. They speak and act and dress differently than the locals. But those long sessions of working together have had their effect. The locals know the newcomers are serious, committed, dedicated. They have their own ways, but they have also learned the ways of the people of the town, and they have worked out . . . a rough and ready friendship. . . . Making something together breaks down walls of suspicion and misunderstanding. . . . That is society as *the home we build together.*[2]

Connections

1. How has migration changed your community? What might you find on the streets today that would not have been there without immigrants?

2. How do newcomers learn to adapt to their new communities? To what extent should they have to change their lives, habits, and customs to fit in? Visiting Germany in February 2008, Turkish Prime Minister Tayyip Erdogan encouraged an audience of Turkish immigrants to integrate in German society but stressed that they should resist assimilation. He proclaimed assimilation "a crime against humanity." What do you think he meant? What is the difference between assimilation and integration?

3. Sacks offers three parables as metaphors for types of integration. What is the moral he is trying to teach?

4. Have you been a guest at someone's home? At a hotel? What is the difference? To what extent do any of these models of integration represent how immigrants are treated in your community? Which model do you prefer? Why?

5. Some critics have suggested that Sacks's three models fail to acknowledge the dangers of terrorism and extremist ideology. The transit bombings in London and Madrid gave rise to concerns that newcomers may have ideas and values that are dangerous and cannot

be integrated. How do you think Sacks would respond to those concerns? How should those concerns influence the way people think about the best way to integrate newcomers? What should communities do if migrants break the rules of their new community?

6. Why do you think Sacks advocates for the third parable, *the home we build together*? What does he see as the advantages of that model? Why does Sacks believe the third model "won't always be easy"? Do you agree? What can be done by either host communities or newcomers to foster integration?

◇ ◇ ◇

Excerpted from *The Home We Build Together*, by permission of the author. Copyright © 2001 by Chief Rabbi Jonathan Sacks.

---

[1] Marcelo Suárez-Orozco, "What Do We Do with Difference in a Globalizing World?" (lecture, Facing History and Ourselves, Brookline, MA, August 11, 2005).

[2] Jonathan Sacks, *The Home We Build Together* (New York: Continuum, 2008), 14–15.

What Is a Nation?

"The migration of people between one nation and another is challenging long-held assumptions about who belongs."

M erriam-Webster's dictionary defines a nation as:

a) a politically organized nationality . . .

b) a community of people composed of one or more nationalities and possessing a more or less defined territory and government

c) a territorial division containing a body of people of one or more nationalities and usually characterized by relatively large size and independent status.

In his influential 1882 essay "What Is a Nation?" French philosopher Ernest Renan wrote about the bonds that hold nations together. He explained, "A heroic past, great men, glory [are the links between people] upon which one bases a national idea. . . . A nation is . . . a large-scale solidarity, constituted by the feeling of sacrifices that one has made in the past and of those that one is prepared to make in the future."[1] Others have stressed language, ethnicity, or even pseudo-scientific ideas about "race." The migration of people between one nation and another is challenging long-held assumptions about who belongs.

The way that many nations officially recognize that people belong is by allowing them to become citizens. In some countries, such as the United States, all individuals who are born in the country are considered citizens regardless of their parents' country of origin. Other countries have different requirements for citizenship. The Germans traditionally defined their nation by race and genealogy. That is, German citizens were part of the *Volk*—a community that linked blood and citizenship. The idea of the German *Volk* was notoriously celebrated by the Nazis and used to justify the persecution

This reading contains excerpts from Roger Cohen's, "Berlin Journal; Poking Fun, Artfully, at a Heady German Word," in the *New York Times*.

and murder of Jews, Gypsies* (Sinti and Roma), and others. In 2004, however, the German Parliament passed a law allowing for *naturalization*, whereby German-born children of immigrants could apply for German citizenship on the basis of residence, work, and other criteria. As a result, some of Germany's approximately 2.3 million Turkish residents were able to become citizens. The hope is that as immigrants become citizens they will become more integrated into society. Will allowing immigrants to become citizens change the identity of the German nation?

▲ The Reichstag in Berlin. The inscription reads, "Dem Deutschen Volke" ("To the German People").

As the changes to Germany's citizenship law were being debated, artist Hans Haacke was invited to submit a proposal for a project housed in the German Parliament building, the Reichstag. Echoing the famous

---

*At the time of the Holocaust, Germans and other non-Roma Europeans used the name "Gypsies" when referring to the ethnic group of people who referred to themselves as Roma. Thus, to avoid historical anachronism, for the lesson plans in this book we use the word "Gypsies" when identifying the groups of people who were targeted for segregation and annihilation by the Nazis. Since the Holocaust, the derogatory qualities of the label "Gypsy" have been recognized, and Roma is considered the more respectful term. Refer to the following websites for more information about the Roma people and their history: *www.rcmani.org, www.religioustolerance.org.*

inscription on the front of the building—"To the German People"—Haacke called his project "To the Population." His project soon became the focus of a debate about citizenship and German national identity.

Roger Cohen wrote about the debate for the *New York Times.*

On the western facade of the Reichstag is an old inscription: "Dem Deutschen Volke"—"To the German People." Straightforward enough. But just how charged and divisive those words are has been revealed by an outcry over a proposed work of art for the refurbished parliamentary building.

The problem . . . is who Germans are. Are they still a "Volk"? The word is associated with identity-through-blood, was debased by Hitler with his clamor of "Fuhrer, Volk und Vaterland [fatherland]" and was further tarnished by the pervasive "Volkspolizei" [secret police] of the East German Communist dictatorship.

Or, with seven million foreigners in their midst and as many restaurants offering "Turkish doner kebab" as wurst, have Germans moved beyond a "volkisch" appreciation of nationality to a more embracing view of the German soul?

That is the central question posed by the work that Hans Haacke, a German artist living in New York, has proposed for the northern courtyard of the Reichstag. Above a trough filled with earth from throughout Germany would appear the illuminated words "Der Bevolkerung" — "To the Population."

. . . The "Volk," of course, is composed of German citizens. The "Bevolkerung" includes the 2.2 million Turks, more than 800,000 people from the former Yugoslavia, more than 600,000 Italians and many others who live here.

Members of the German Parliament put soil from their local communities into Hans Haacke's controversial art piece "To the Population." ▶

AP Photo/Markus Schreiber

. . . The uproar reflects just how sensitive the issue of German identity remains, even after the approval last year of a law making it easier for immigrants and their children to obtain citizenship. The suggestion that Germany is a "land of immigration," a notion strongly supported by the facts, still stirs widespread unease or anger.

. . . Peter Ramsauer and many other conservative members of Parliament . . . believe "This is political art, a provocative attempt to portray the words on the facade of the Reichstag as nationalistic," he said. "But 'Volk' is just a normal word; it's ridiculous to think Hitler tainted it forever. German history is more than the 12 Nazi years."

. . . In a telephone interview, Mr. Haacke conceded that the word "Volk" has had some "good meanings" over the years. But he argued that it was also charged with ominous connotations, thanks to the Nazis and the East German leadership. To the artist, the word reeks of myth, of tribes, of blood lines, of all that Germany should now shun.[2]

Connections

1. What is a nation? How does a nation get its identity? From its people? From its past? From its laws? From shared experiences? How do national identities change over time? To what extent do nations have a permanent culture? Should they have one?

2. How did Renan define a nation? What did he believe gives a nation its identity? Compare his ideas with yours and those of your classmates.

3. When scholars discuss nations and national identity, many try to identify the "social glue" that serves as a bond between different groups and people within a nation. What ideas and experiences serve as the social glue for your community? For your country?

4. Why do you think people see immigration as a challenge to national identity? What does this suggest about how people understand the concept of "nation"?

5. In his project for the German Parliament building, the Reichstag, Haacke reworked the famous phrase "To the German People" (or *Volk*) and made it "To the Population." Why do you think Haacke felt it was important to change the words? How does his rephrasing change the meaning? What does it suggest about his vision for the future of Germany?

6. For many, the word *Volk* is associated with National Socialism and the Holocaust. How can countries signal to their populations and the rest of the world that they are working to create a more inclusive national identity and culture?

7. In your own country, who do you think the phrase "my country's people" refers to? Who would be included in "the population of my country" or "the people who live in my country"? Are there differences between these characterizations? If so, what does each phrase imply? Do you think these differences are useful or problematic?

◇ ◇ ◇

---

[1] Ernest Renan, "What Is a Nation?" as quoted in Geoff Eley & Ronald Grigor Suny, *Becoming National. A Reader* (New York: Oxford University Press, 1996), 52–4.

[2] Roger Cohen, "Berlin Journal; Poking Fun, Artfully, at a Heady German Word." the *New York Times*, March 31, 2000, *http://query.nytimes.com/gst/fullpage.html?res=9D0CE5D9123CF932A05750C0A9669 C8B63&scp=3&sq=Roger+Cohen+Reichstag* (accessed January 9, 2008).

National Pride

"Cohesive communities are places where '[t]here is a clearly defined and widely shared sense of the contribution of different individuals and communities to a future vision for a neighborhood, city, region, or country.'"

Many politicians and community members fear that with increased immigration, neighborhoods will develop into "parallel societies" divided along ethnic lines. In an interview, Seyran Ates, a Turkish-German women's rights activist, explains her concern that Germany is becoming "two societies with two different value systems living side by side, but separate from one another."[1]

In response to a similar debate in Britain, the Commission on Integration published a report on what it called "Community Cohesion." According to the report, cohesive communities are places where "[t]here is a clearly defined and widely shared sense of the contribution of different individuals and communities to a future vision for a neighborhood, city, region, or country."[2]

A number of people in Britain have worked to celebrate an inclusive vision of British identity that they hope will contribute to more cohesive communities. This issue has become more important given the heated political discussion about immigration, diversity, and proper responses to religious extremism. Contributing to the dialogue, former attorney general Lord Peter Goldsmith presented proposals in March 2008 for a number of ceremonies, including a pledge of allegiance, designed to invoke pride in a common British identity that embraces diversity. This raised concerns that such efforts will promote nationalism and alienate people who don't think of themselves as only British. The following is an excerpt from the *International Herald Tribune* describing the response.

This reading contains excerpts from the *International Herald Tribune*.

The idea sounds simple: build British pride with a new pledge of allegiance, a new national holiday, and citizenship ceremonies for school children and immigrants.

But the report ordered up by British Prime Minister Gordon Brown, which calls for [the] introduction of a number of American-style patriotic rituals, raises thorny questions in the sometimes fractious United Kingdom.

▲ Britain's Queen Elizabeth II greets a line of schoolchildren waving Union Jacks in Aylesbury, England.

For starters, are people in Wales, Scotland and Northern Ireland who seek more independence anxious to pledge their allegiance to a united country? And will republicans who want an end to Britain's monarchy really offer undying devotion to queen and country?

. . . The public response to Goldsmith's plan was mixed. Some people questioned in central London welcomed it as a way to show national pride; others said a pledge would not have any impact.

Carla Jordan, a third-year law student at the University of Exeter, said the plan would help schoolchildren understand what it means to be British. . . . "I'm quite for people having a more patriotic outlook on their country," she said. "I think it's a good thing. I don't think a lot of people understand British values or what they stand for and I think if children were taught them it would help."

But sales manager Paul Hughes said instituting a pledge of allegiance would not have an effect on the slow rate of integration by new groups of immigrants that he believes is an underlying problem facing Britain. . . . "People aren't bad because they don't like the queen or pledge allegiance to the queen," he said. "But what they've got to do is work within the confines of English law and support the structure of U.K. law and integrate into society."

Phil Thomas, a systems administrator in London, said he doubts that adding a pledge of allegiance would have much impact. . . . "I think people think of themselves as being English or Welsh or Scottish or Irish," he said. "I don't think there's a great national identity."

In his report, Goldsmith said he was not trying to set policy for how many immigrants should be admitted to the U.K. . . but was looking for ways that new arrivals could be given a better sense of belonging in their new home.[3]

Connections

1. Consider the British government's definition of "community cohesion." Why do you think the British government is concerned with developing a shared vision or identity? Should community cohesion be a goal?

2. What do you think a cohesive community would look like? What activities support community cohesion? What parts of that definition might you apply to your community? What can be done to support cohesion in your community?

3. Why do you think some people view an emphasis on Britishness as an important way to integrate newcomers? Do you think such efforts help or hinder integration?

4. What is the difference between patriotism and nationalism? What do you think of the proposal to create a new pledge of allegiance, a national holiday, and citizenship ceremonies for schools and immigrants? Can pledges, holidays, and education help to reinforce an inclusive collective identity? What are some ways to promote patriotism without alienating immigrants?

5. If you were to write a pledge of allegiance for your community, what would it say? If you were to create a holiday to celebrate a national identity, what kind of activities and rituals would you include?

6. What can leaders and governments do to reinforce a sense of common belonging? When does attention to differences break down a sense of common identity?

◇ ◇ ◇

Reprinted by permission from the Associated Press (March 11, 2008).

---

[1] Sylvia Poggioli, "In Europe, Muslim Women Face Multiple Issues," *NPR*, January 20, 2008, *http://www.npr.org/templates/story/story.php?storyId=18234876* (accessed January 25, 2008).

[2] Commission on Integration and Cohesion, "Our Shared Future," June 14, 2007, *http://www.integrationandcohesion.org.uk/upload/assets/www.integrationandcohesion.org.uk/our_shared_future.pdf* (accessed November 6, 2007).

[3] "New proposal for British pledge of allegiance and citizenship ceremony sparks opposition," the *International Herald Tribune*, March 11, 2008, *http://www.iht.com/bin/printfriendly.php?id=10919759* (accessed March 11, 2008).

◇ ◇ ◇

Dilemmas of Integration

◇ ◇ ◇

Identity in Diaspora

"Stories are like these onions—like dried experience. They aren't the original experience but they are more than nothing at all. You think about a story, you turn it over in your mind, and it becomes something else."

Today, increasing numbers of people are living outside of their ancestral homelands. Many immigrants fear that their children will assimilate into their new home and lose their connection to their cultural identity. How do people learn the history of their group and their culture when that group is spread around the world? Can rituals, memories, and stories replace a physical community? In her memoir, *The Storyteller's Daughter*, Saira Shah recalls listening to her father's magical tales while the two of them cooked together in their British kitchen, surrounded by the smells of Afghani spices rising from their pots. She writes:

My father understood the value of stories: he was a writer. My parents had picked Kent as an idyllic place to bring up their children, but we were never allowed to forget our Afghan background.

Periodically during my childhood, my father would come upon the kitchen like a storm. . . .

During these cookery sessions, we played a wonderful game. We planned the family trip to Afghanistan that always seemed to be just round the corner. How we would go back to Paghman, stroll in the gardens, visit our old family home and greet the relatives we had never met. When we arrived in the Paghman mountains, the men would fire their guns in the air—we shouldn't worry, that was the Afghan way of welcome and celebration. They would carry us on their

This reading contains excerpts from Saira Shah's, *The Storyteller's Daughter: One Woman's Return to Her Lost Homeland.*

Giorgio Scarlini/Getty Images

▲ Pilau with pomegranate seeds and pistachios

shoulders, whooping and cheering, and in the evening we would eat a *pilau** that eclipsed even the great feasts of the court of our ancestors.

My mother's family background, which is Parsee from India, rarely got a look in. As far as my father was concerned, his off-spring were pure Afghan. For years, the mere mention of the Return was enough to stoke us children into fits of excitement. It was so much more alluring than our mundane Kentish lives, which revolved round the family's decrepit Land Rover and our pet Labrador, Honey.

. . . When I was fifteen, the Soviet Union invaded and occupied Afghanistan. During a *pilau*-making session quite soon after that, I voiced an anxiety that had been growing for some time now. How could my father expect us to be truly Afghan when we had grown up outside an Afghan community? When we went back home, wouldn't we children be strangers, foreign-ers in our own land? I expected, and possibly hoped for, the

---

* *Pilau* is a Middle Eastern, Central and South Asian rice dish often spiced with saffron.

soothing account of our triumphant and imminent return to Paghman. It didn't come. My father looked tired and sad. His answer startled me: "I've given you stories to replace a community. They are your community."

"But surely stories can't replace experience."

He picked up a packet of dehydrated onion. "Stories are like these onions—like dried experience. They aren't the original experience but they are more than nothing at all. You think about a story, you turn it over in your mind, and it becomes something else." He added hot water to the onion. "It's not fresh onion—fresh experience—but it is something that can help you to recognize experience when you come across it. Experiences follow patterns, which repeat themselves again and again. In our tradition, stories can help you recognize the shape of an experience, to make sense of and to deal with it. So, you see, what you may take for mere snippets of myth and legend encapsulate what you need to know to guide you on your way anywhere among Afghans."

"Well, as soon as I'm eighteen I'm going to go to see for myself," I said, adding craftily: "Then perhaps I'll have some fresh experiences that will help me grow up."

My father had been swept along on the tide of his analogy. Now, he suddenly became a parent whose daughter was at an impressionable age and whose country was embroiled in a murderous war.

"If you would only grow up a little in the first place," he snapped, "then you would realize that you don't need to go at all."[1]

Connections

1. The word *diaspora* comes from the Greek word for scattering seeds. Today the term refers to people who are living outside of their ancestral homeland. Do you consider yourself part of a diaspora? If so, how does this shape the way you define yourself? Do you know others living in a diaspora?

2. How do people living in a diaspora retain their identity? What are the challenges they face?

3. Why do you think it was important to Shah's father that his children see themselves as Afghan even if he never intended for them to go to Afghanistan?

4. Shah's father uses a metaphor of dried onions to describe the importance of storytelling in the Afghan culture. To what extent does he believe that stories can create a community? Are there stories that are important in your culture? What are they supposed to teach members of your group? Do they influence the way you see yourself?

5. Interview members of your family about the stories that were passed down to them about their culture. What values and lessons were these stories supposed to teach?

◇ ◇ ◇

---

[1] Saira Shah, *The Storyteller's Daughter: One Woman's Return to Her Lost Homeland* (New York: First Anchor Books, 2003), 5–7.

Transcultural Identities

"Like many immigrant offspring I felt intense pressure to be two things, loyal to the old world and fluent in the new, approved of on either side of the hyphen."

Cultural psychologist Carola Suárez-Orozco writes that for children, "the task of immigration . . . is creating a transcultural identity." She explains, "These youth must creatively fuse aspects of two or more cultures—the parental tradition and the new culture or cultures. In so doing, they synthesize an identity that does not require them to choose between cultures but incorporates traits of both cultures."[1]

Like many immigrants to Europe, Indian-American author Jhumpa Lahiri has lived in two cultures for most of her life. Balancing her dual identity has not always been easy for her. Despite her rich heritage, while growing up, she never felt completely Indian or American. Only later in life did she accept both of her identities. Lahiri, now a parent, hopes to pass both of her identities on to her children. She explains:

> I have lived in the United States for almost 37 years and anticipate growing old in this country. Therefore, with the exception of my first two years in London, "Indian-American" has been a constant way to describe me. Less constant is my relationship to the term. When I was growing up in Rhode Island in the 1970s I felt neither Indian nor American. Like many immigrant offspring I felt intense pressure to be two things, loyal to the old world and fluent in the new, approved of on either side of the hyphen. Looking back, I see that this was generally the case. But my perception as a young girl was that I fell short at both ends, shuttling between two dimensions that had nothing to do with one another.

This reading contains excerpts from Jhumpa Lahiri's, "My Two Lives," *Newsweek World News.*

At home I followed the customs of my parents, speaking Bengali and eating rice and *dal** with my fingers. These ordinary facts seemed part of a secret, utterly alien way of life, and I took pains to hide them from my American friends. For my parents, home was not our house in Rhode Island but Calcutta, where they were raised. I was aware that

▲ Author Jhumpa Lahiri and her family

Amanda Edwards/Getty Images

the things they lived for—the Nazrul songs they listened to on the reel-to-reel, the family they missed, the clothes my mother wore that were not available in any store in any mall—were at once as precious and as worthless as an outmoded currency.

I also entered a world my parents had little knowledge or control of: school, books, music, television, things that seeped in and became a fundamental aspect of who I am. I spoke English without an accent, comprehending the language in a way my parents still do not. And yet there was evidence that I was not entirely American. In addition to my distinguishing name and looks, I did not attend Sunday school, did not know how to ice-skate, and disappeared to India for months at a time. Many of my friends proudly called themselves Irish-American or Italian-American. But they were several generations removed from the frequently humiliating process of immigration, so that the ethnic roots they claimed had descended underground whereas mine were still tangled and green. According to my parents I was not American, nor would I ever be no matter

---

* *Dal* is an Indian term for all varieties of dried beans, split peas, and lentils.

how hard I tried. I felt doomed by their pronouncement, misunderstood and gradually defiant. In spite of the first lessons of arithmetic, one plus one did not equal two but zero, my conflicting selves always canceling each other out.

. . . As I approach middle age, one plus one equals two, both in my work and in my daily existence. The traditions on either side of the hyphen dwell in me like siblings, still occasionally sparring, one outshining the other depending on the day. But like siblings they are intimately familiar with one another, forgiving and intertwined. When my husband and I were married five years ago in Calcutta we invited friends who had never been to India, and they came full of enthusiasm for a place I avoided talking about in my childhood, fearful of what people might say. Around non-Indian friends, I no longer feel compelled to hide the fact that I speak another language. I speak Bengali to my children, even though I lack the proficiency to teach them to read or write the language. As a child I sought perfection and so denied myself the claim to any identity. As an adult I accept that a bicultural upbringing is a rich but imperfect thing.

While I am American by virtue of the fact that I was raised in this country, I am Indian thanks to the efforts of two individuals. I feel Indian not because of the time I've spent in India or because of my genetic composition but rather because of my parents' steadfast presence in my life. . . .

I have always believed that I lack the authority my parents bring to being Indian. But as long as they live they protect me from feeling like an impostor. Their passing will mark not only the loss of the people who created me but the loss of a singular way of life, a singular struggle. The immigrant's journey, no matter how ultimately rewarding, is founded on departure and deprivation, but it secures for the subsequent generation a sense of arrival and advantage. I can see a day coming when my American side, lacking the counterpoint India has until now maintained, begins to gain ascendancy and weight. It is in fiction that I will continue to interpret the term "Indian-American," calculating that shifting equation, whatever answers it may yield.[2]

Connections

1. What does Suárez-Orozsco mean when she says "the task of immigration . . . is creating a transcultural identity"? How was Lahiri able to "fuse" aspects of her Indian identity with her identity as an American?

2. Lahiri writes, "Like many immigrant offspring I felt intense pressure to be two things, loyal to the old world and fluent in the new, approved of on either side of the hyphen." Why is there pressure to choose between her two identities? Do people have to choose one identity?

3. Lahiri talks about the Indian customs she followed at home with her parents. She explains, "These ordinary facts seemed part of a secret, utterly alien way of life, and I took pains to hide them from my American friends. . . . According to my parents I was not American, nor would I ever be no matter how hard I tried . . . one plus one did not equal two but zero, my conflicting selves always canceling each other out." What do you think Lahiri means? Why do you think she felt she had to hide her identity? Are there times when you hide parts of who you are?

4. Lahiri worries she lacks the "authority" to be Indian. Why? What authority does a person need to belong to a group? Who determines which people belong to a group and which people don't belong?

Lahiri's novel *The Namesake* recounts the story of an Indian immigrant family in the United States in the 1970s. The book became the subject of a feature film by the same name. Her short-story collections *Interpreter of Maladies* and *Unaccustomed Earth* reflect on the themes of immigration, identity, and the impact of these experiences on families.

◇ ◇ ◇

Excerpted from *Newsweek* (March 2006).

---

[1] Carola Suárez-Orozco, "Formulating Identity in a Globalized World," *Globalization: Culture and Education in the New Millennium*, ed. Marcelo Suárez-Orozco and Qin-Hilliard (Berkeley: University of California Press, 2004), 192.

[2] Jhumpa Lahiri, "My Two Lives," *Newsweek World News*, *http://www.msnbc.msn.com/id/11569225/site/newsweek/* (accessed May 23, 2007).

Jews in Europe

"[For Jews,] [t]here was a long struggle to define an identity both British and Jewish. But these are pains of adjustment, not permanent conditions."

Until recently, Jews were the largest non-Christian religious minority in Europe. Like other religious minorities today, they have often had to prove their loyalty to the countries where they live. Their struggles reveal the profound challenges religious minorities face as they work to be accepted while also maintaining their identity. While Jewish history in Europe is marked by stories of individual accomplishments, it is also scarred by a long and brutal history of antisemitism and the Holocaust.

During the French Revolution, France became the first European nation to offer Jews citizenship. After the revolution, Napoleon, then the emperor of France, gathered 71 rabbis and other Jewish leaders to discuss the following questions. Napoleon was concerned that Jews would not be loyal to the French Republic. He asked:

In the eyes of Jews, are Frenchmen considered as their brethren? Or are they considered as strangers? Do Jews born in France, and treated by the laws as French citizens, consider France their country?

The Jews Napoleon questioned responded:

The love of country is in the heart of Jews a sentiment so natural, so powerful, and so constant to their religious opinions, that a French Jew considered himself in England, as among

This reading contains excerpts from Jonathan Sacks's, "Giving and Belonging: the lesson Jews can offer new immigrants," *Times Online*.

strangers, although he may be among Jews; and the case is the same with English Jews in France.

To such a pitch is this sentiment carried among them, that during the last war, French Jews have been seen fighting desperately against other Jews, the subjects of countries then at war with France.[1]

Napoleon responded by officially recognizing Judaism as a religion in France along with Catholicism, Lutheranism, and Calvinism. Despite outbreaks of antisemitism and the systematic murder of nearly a quarter of France's Jewish population during the Holocaust, today France is home to the largest Jewish population in Europe. Britain has the second largest Jewish community in Europe. In 2005, Jews celebrated the 350th anniversary of Jewish life in Britain. Although they still face discrimination, Jews are no longer the largest religious minority in Britain. Today's newcomers arrive from Asia and Africa; they are Hindus, Sikhs, and Muslims. Writing in the *Times* of London, the Chief Rabbi of the British Commonwealth, Jonathan Sacks, considers the history of Jewish immigration to England and its implications for immigrants today.

The Jews who came here were asylum-seekers from successive waves of persecution. The first were descendants of the victims of the Spanish and Portuguese expulsions. My late father came to find refuge from anti-Semitism in Poland. Some

▲ A German Jewish refugee in England, 1938

© Hulton-Deutsch Collection/Corbis

came through Kindertransport, the British effort to save Jewish children from Nazi Germany. Others arrived as survivors of the Holocaust.

It wasn't always easy to be Jewish in Britain. It took 200 years before Jews were permitted to enter universities or be elected to Parliament. Jewish immigrants—poor, concentrated in ghettoes, barely able to speak English—were caricatured as alien elements in British life. Jews who remember those days can readily sympathise with Hindus, Sikhs and Muslims today.

Within an astonishingly short time, they were full participants in British society. . . . There is a message of hope here for other ethnic and religious minorities. Integration and acceptance don't happen overnight. And yes, there were conflicts between immigrant parents and their British-born and educated children. There was a long struggle to define an identity both British and Jewish. But these are pains of adjustment, not permanent conditions.

The Jewish experience challenges the received wisdom about minorities. Jews did not seek multiculturalism. They sought to integrate, adapt and belong. Jewish schools focused on turning Jews into British citizens, at home in the nation's language, culture and history. Sermons were spiced with quotations from [British writers] Shakespeare, Milton and Wordsworth. . . .

Britain was different in those days. . . . It had the quiet confidence of a nation secure in its own identity. It remembered . . . that for minorities to integrate there must be something for them to integrate into. Subtly and with a certain grace, Britain reminded Jews that there were rules, things you did and didn't do. I remember Bertha Leverton, one of the children saved from Germany in 1939, telling of how she was taught, on her first day in England, that it was polite to leave some food uneaten on the side of your plate. She was starving and traumatised, yet the gesture helped to make her feel at home. She appreciated the hidden message: from here on, you are one of us.

For the first time in my life, Jews feel uncomfortable in Britain. They have heard public figures making crude gibes about Jews. They have seen Holocaust Memorial Day—dedicated to all victims of man's inhumanity to man—misrepresented and politicised. Throughout Europe, Jewish students are harassed, synagogues vandalised and cemeteries desecrated. These things matter not because of the threat they pose to Jews, but because anti-Semitism is always an advance warning of a wider crisis.[2]

Connections

1. Napoleon questioned whether it was possible to be both Jewish and French. This question is relevant for religious minorities today. Do religious and national identities necessarily conflict? Can they complement each other?

2. What point were Jewish leaders trying to make in response to Napoleon's question?

3. Are there some groups that have been pressured more than others to prove their loyalty in your community? Why do you think this happens?

4. Why do some people wonder whether it is possible to be a religious minority—and feel deep solidarity with other members of their religion around the world—and also be full citizens of a nation at the same time? Do the two identities conflict?

5. Sacks shares his insights about the Jewish experience in Britain. What does he hope others will learn from this history?

6. Sacks believes that "for minorities to integrate, there must be something for them to integrate into." What does he mean? Do you agree? What is the difference between integration and assimilation?

7. Sacks describes the way that Bertha Leverton was welcomed into British culture. How are newcomers welcomed into your community? How do newcomers know they belong?

8. What does Sacks mean when he says, "anti-Semitism is always an advance warning of a wider crisis"? Human rights monitoring groups have documented a rise in antisemitic words and actions in Europe in recent years.[3] What do you think this means for Jews and other minorities in Europe? What can communities do to respond to antisemitism? How do you think antisemitism affects Jewish identity?

Like all diaspora communities, Jews have struggled to maintain their identity and culture in the face of prejudice and pressure to conform to community expectations. However, there is not one way to be Jewish, just as there is not one way to be a member of most groups. To explore Jewish identity in diaspora further, see the film *The Jewish Americans*. Copies of the film are available in the Facing History and Ourselves library. Go to *www.facinghistory.org* for more information.

◇ ◇ ◇

Reprinted from *Times Online* (October 1, 2005) by permission of the author. Copyright © 2005 by Chief Rabbi Jonathan Sacks.

---

[1] The Assembly of Jewish Notables, "Answers to Napoleon," *http://www.ucalgary.ca/~elsegal/363_Transp/Sanhedrin.html* (accessed January 25, 2008).

[2] Jonathan Sacks, "Giving and Belonging: the lesson Jews can offer new immigrants," *Times Online*, October 1, 2005, *http://www.timesonline.co.uk/tol/comment/columnists/guest_contributors/article573244.ece* (accessed January 25, 2008).

³ According to the European Monitoring Centre on Racism and Xenophobia, "Antisemitism is a certain perception of Jews, which may be expressed as hatred toward Jews. . . . Antisemitism frequently charges Jews with conspiring to harm humanity, and it is often used to blame Jews for 'why things go wrong.' It is expressed in speech, writing, visual forms, and action, and employs sinister stereotypes and negative character traits." The European Union Agency for Fundamental Rights, "Working Definition of Antisemitism," http://fra.europa.eu/fra/material/pub/AS/AS-WorkingDefinition-draft.pdf (accessed September 19, 2007).

From Foreigners to Muslims

"This second generation does not feel at home anywhere else than in Germany. Yet the society in which they live largely rejects them and places them within the Muslim group, which is regarded as a homogeneous entity."

Once, Jews were the most visible religious minority in Europe; today it is Muslims. As is true for any religious group, not all Muslims are the same. Groups are created and defined both by their members and by how others perceive them. Those attitudes, from within and without, influence the identities of both the group and its individual members. Riem Spielhaus, a scholar of Islamic studies, researches Muslim group identity in Germany. Spielhaus traces the way politicians, the public, and the press talk about migrants in Germany. She writes that in these discussions of identity, immigrants or "foreigners" have increasingly been labeled "Muslims." This has affected not only the way non-Muslims view immigrants from Muslim countries, but also the way people from Muslim backgrounds view themselves—regardless of their religious practice. Spielhaus believes that the emphasis on the religious identity of migrants and their families has implications for the integration of Muslims into German society. Spielhaus explains:

For decades the religion of immigrants was not an issue in Germany. However, in the country's present discourse on Muslims their religious identity is often emphasized. This has led to the construction of a Muslim community in Germany . . . while the ethnic, religious and cultural diversity of Muslims is not recognized.

This reading contains excerpts from Riem Spielhaus's, "Religion and Identity: How Germany's foreigners have become Muslims," *Internationale Politik*.

▲ The Sehitlik Mosque on Open Mosque Day in Berlin, Germany

Although large numbers of Muslims from an array of countries have been living in Germany since the 1970s, it was not until the 1990s that migrants' religious affiliations and practices were noted by academia, politics and the broader public. Until then research on guest workers and refugees living in Germany focused on living conditions, schooling, memories of the homeland, and migration experiences. Religious affiliation was rarely considered. It was only in the 1990s that the first studies were undertaken on Islamic organizations and religiosity; twenty years after guest workers had begun to establish mosque associations and started to petition state governments and municipal authorities on matters of religious import. It took the public discourse even longer to recognize Muslims as such, rather than as foreigners whose stay in Germany was expected to be simply temporary. In fact, a debate on integration was first initiated after a consensus was reached over migrants' right to remain in Germany permanently and become full-fledged members of society.

...Until then many Germans believed that the majority of the immigrants would return to their countries of origin. This was indeed the goal of many guestworker families as well; they had invested their savings in houses and apartments in the old country and dreamed of an eventual return. Only slowly did they realize that for their children who had grown up in Germany this was hardly a viable option. This second generation does not feel at home anywhere else than in Germany. Yet the society in which they live largely rejects them and places them within the Muslim group, which is regarded as a homogeneous entity.

...The public's growing realization that Islamic culture in Europe is here to stay has led to a shift in perception—these "foreigners" did not become Germans but are now seen as "Muslims." Religious affiliation thus gained importance in the discourse. However, the vehemence of this development seems only understandable . . . in the aftermath of 9/11. Whereas before 2000 [when German citizenship law allowed migrants to become citizens] social problems relating to migrants were discussed while applying the categories "foreigner" and "Turk," today the observations spotlight their— often only assumed—religious affiliation. . . . Religion thereby becomes the pattern for explaining both positive but especially negative social behavior. This obscures the more complex reality that religion is neither the only nor the most important identity for the majority of Muslims, and it is certainly not the only reason for their actions.[1]

Spielhaus believes that one of the challenges Muslims in Germany face is that:

Individuals from Muslim countries are forever being confronted with the question of religious affiliation. An example

of this is the innumerable requests made of prominent figures of Turkish, Arab or Iranian descent to take a position on
nearly every Islam-related occurrence. . . . It is simply taken for
granted that individuals of Muslim heritage are Muslim, religious and different . . .

Until recently, Spielhaus explains that for migrants:

. . . National, ethnic and language barriers have . . . been
stronger than the community feeling in their organizations
and in daily life. For first-generation Muslims, their identity
is frequently inseparable from their nation of origin. . . . But
unity is slowly increasing between German converts to Islam
and second- and third-generation immigrants who have
reinvented the idea of the unity of Muslims, the umma, in
Germany . . . despite ethnic, national differences. . . .

The increasing use of antagonistic categories [in Germany]
such as "you" and "we," "our culture" and "your community"
do[es] not support integration. . . . The search for a German
identity and the process of integration is hindered by stereotypes that serve to depict this process as condemned to
failure or having in fact already failed. . . . It is inadequate to
simply look for the roots of problems in Islam or to ask
Muslim organizations to take responsibility for them. Diverse
strategies are necessary to ensure complete integration and
so as to secure participation in the democratic process for all
immigrants and their children in general and for Muslims in
particular.[2]

Connections

1. How do the perceptions of others shape the way groups define their identities? How does group identity shape the identity of individuals who belong? How does Spielhaus relate these ideas to the creation of a Muslim identity in Germany? What can both Muslims and non-Muslims do to influence the way people think about Muslims as a group?

2. Spielhaus explains that perceptions about group identity have implications for integration. For example, she notes that after the changes in the German citizenship laws, "these 'foreigners' [from Muslim majority countries] did not become Germans but are now seen as 'Muslims.'" What is the difference between those labels? How do they reflect different ideas about identity?

3. What makes someone a Muslim? Is it a matter of religious beliefs, religious practice, family background, culture, or something else? How do you think fear of extremism influences the way people are answering that question?

4. Writing about the treatment of Muslims in the United Kingdom, columnist Gary Younge writes that many people can define their own identity, but what is happening now in the West is forcing all Muslims to be defined by their religious identity. He explains:

> We have a choice about which identities to give to the floor [to highlight] . . . ; but at specific moments, they may also choose us. Where Muslim identity in the west is concerned, that moment is now. . . .[3]

Why is this happening now? To what extent do his comments apply to other groups, as well?

5. How do others define the group or groups that you belong to? Does it match the way you see the group?

Reprinted from *Internationale Politik* (Spring 2006) by permission of the publisher.

[1] Riem Spielhaus, "Religion and Identity: How Germany's foreigners have become Muslims," *Internationale Politik* (Spring 2006), *http://www.fulbright.de/fileadmin/files/togermany/information/2005–06/gss/TIP_0206_Spielhaus.pdf* (accessed March 5, 2008).

[2] Ibid.

[3] Gary Younge, "We can choose our identity, but sometimes it also chooses us," the *Guardian*, January 21, 2005, *http://www.guardian.co.uk/uk/2005/jan/21/islamandbritain.comment7* (accessed March 5, 2008).

Searching for an Identity

"At the heart of the disillusionment that many of my friends felt was not knowing how they fitted into British society. I wasn't immune, either. At 19, I found myself becoming increasingly drawn to Islam. I was struck, when I visited Pakistan, by the confidence of the people, who seemed comfortable in their own skins in a way that my friends and I were not."

Yasmin Hai is part of a generation of migrants who grew up in England. Like many of her peers, Hai was encouraged by her Pakistani parents to assimilate. Despite her efforts, however, she felt that she would never truly fit into British culture. In the excerpt below, Hai writes about her own search for identity and the different choices some of her friends have made. Some people of Hai's generation, like her friend Nazia, were attracted to religious communities, where they found a new sense of belonging and purpose. Sometimes, though, these religious communities were appealing because they were so critical of the broader society, advocating rejection of British culture and values. As Hai says,

Muslim girl eating cotton candy in East London. ▶

This reading contains excerpts from Yasmin Hai's, "Revenge of the young Muslims," *Times Online*.

When my friend Nazia started flirting with Islam, I felt betrayed. Over the years, we had been clubbing together and got up to all sorts of mischief. Now she was abandoning me.

I wasn't bothered that she'd started praying five times a day. . . . But when she started denigrating Western culture, I felt that she'd betrayed me, herself and our entire Asian community.

I'd grown up in suburban Wembley in a strongly Asian area. My father, who had come to Britain from Pakistan as a political refugee in 1964, was ambitious for his family. So he encouraged my younger brother and sister and me to adopt the ways of the English.

We were banned, for example, from speaking Urdu to our mother: she could speak to us in our mother tongue, but we had to answer in English. Nor were we encouraged to practise Islam. In fact, my father bought me the *Book of Common Prayer* so I wouldn't feel excluded during school assemblies.

Most of my friends were brought up in similar culturally ambiguous households. So when my friend Nazia started using racist terminology, stereotyping white people as cultureless drunks who don't know how to look after their children, I was furious.

We had both gone to university; but while I flourished at Manchester and threw myself into the club scene, she was finding the normal excesses of university life unsettling. It was then that she started to feel that she would never be able to participate fully in English life. After graduating, she agreed to an arranged marriage—her way of reconnecting with the Asian community. But when the marriage failed, the community ostracised her.

This rejection was devastating. At that point, she started to take an interest in the more politicised version of Islam that had begun to filter through in the early 1990s.

Becoming a strict Muslim was her way of exacting revenge on the community that had deserted her when she needed it most.

She wasn't the only one I knew to take that path. For so many of my Asian friends, radical Islam was not so much a matter of being anti-West as a way of wresting back some form of identity. In the early 1990s many of them had thrown themselves into the club and drug scene. Most, though, eventually started to suffer from a creeping form of cultural guilt.

Becoming a committed Muslim was a way of being born again, of wiping the slate clean. You could use your new identity to define yourself against the Western way of life—and against your parents.

As many of us weren't fluent in our mother tongue, and often discouraged from talking about our problems, we hadn't ever had a meaningful dialogue with our parents. My own relationship with my mother suffered immeasurably as a result of this.

. . . At the heart of the disillusionment that many of my friends felt was not knowing how they fitted into British society. I wasn't immune, either. At 19, I found myself becoming increasingly drawn to Islam. I was struck, when I visited Pakistan, by the confidence of the people, who seemed comfortable in their own skins in a way that my friends and I were not.

Here, the chasm that now exists between Asian generations has created a generation of vulnerable young people seeking direction and a sense of belonging. And that makes them more likely to turn to a fundamentalist ideology that professes to offer answers.

. . . In my own case, I realised eventually that I didn't have to force my life into a narrative that had been imposed on it by either British—or radical Islamic—conventional wisdoms. There was nothing wrong with being me.[1]

Connections

1. What insights does Hai offer about her generation's search for identity? How does she reconcile her two identities?

2. Hai writes, "Becoming a committed Muslim was a way of being born again, of wiping the slate clean." Why might some young women of Hai's generation want to wipe the slate clean?

3. Hai says, "Becoming a strict Muslim was [Nazia's] way of exacting revenge on the community that had deserted her when she needed it most." What does she mean? How does Hai explain her friend Nazia's interest in religion? Why does she think Nazia and others like her started to turn against British society?

4. Hai describes a gap between her parents—immigrants from Pakistan—and her generation, which grew up in England. Why do you think Hai feels there is a generation gap? Is there a gap between your parents' generation and yours? How might the experiences of immigrants and their children widen that gap?

◇ ◇ ◇

Reprinted by permission from the *Sunday Times* (April 6, 2008). Copyright © 2008 by Times Online.

[1] Yasmin Hai, "Revenge of the young Muslims," *Times Online*, April 6, 2008, *http://www.timesonline.co.uk/tol/comment/columnists/guest_contributors/article3689767.ece* (accessed May 30, 2008).

Religion and National Identity

"In every democratic and more-or-less secular country . . . questions arise about the precise extent to which religious sub-cultures should be allowed to live by their own rules and 'laws.'"

R eligious diversity is challenging old assumptions about the proper relationship between church and state. In February 2008, the Archbishop of Canterbury, Reverend Rowan Williams sparked an uproar when he suggested that British law should consider incorporating some elements of Islamic law to help foster social cohesion. Many who opposed this idea responded that adapting the law to accommodate diversity would only reinforce the differences between people. An article in the news magazine the *Economist* argued that the controversy reflected a larger tension between secularism, religious diversity, and national identity.

▲ British Prime Minister Gordon Brown (left) and Archbishop of Canterbury Reverend Rowan Williams responding to the controversy over the relationship between sharia and British law

This reading contains excerpts from the *Economist* and the *Guardian*.

In every democratic and more-or-less secular country . . . questions arise about the precise extent to which religious sub-cultures should be allowed to live by their own rules and "laws." One set of questions emerges when believers [of any religion] demand, and often get, an opt-out from the law of the land. Sikhs in British Columbia [a Canadian province] can ride motorcycles without helmets [because otherwise they would cover their turbans]; some are campaigning for the right not to wear hard hats on building sites. Muslims and Jews slaughter animals in ways that others might consider cruel; [some] Catholic doctors and nurses refuse to have anything to do with abortion or euthanasia. . . . What has upset the old equilibrium, say law pundits in several countries, is the emergence all over the world of Muslim minorities who, regardless of what they actually want, are suspected by the rest of society of preparing to establish a "state within a state." . . . The very word *sharia*—which at its broadest can imply a sort of divine ideal about how society should be organised, but can also refer to specific forms of corporal and capital punishment—is now political dynamite.

. . . An uproar began in 2003 when Syed Mumtaz Ali, a retired . . . lawyer, said he was setting up a *sharia* court to settle family law disputes for Muslims [in the Canadian province of Ontario]. Such arrangements were allowed by the province's 1991 Arbitration Act and could carry the force of law.

The proposal caused an instant backlash, right across the religious and political spectrum; many Muslim groups were opposed too. Marion Boyd, a retired attorney-general, investigated the matter and initially recommended that the Arbitration Act should continue to allow disputes to be adjudicated by religious bodies—subject to stricter regulation by the state . . . . In September 2005 the province's premier, Dalton McGuinty, decided to prohibit all settlement of family matters based on religious principles under the Arbitration Act. Religious arbitrators could still offer services in the settlement of disputes, but their rulings would not have legal effect or be enforceable by the courts. The province's laws were duly changed.

. . . Defining the relationship between religion and the state was certainly easier when it could be assumed that religion's hold over people's lives and behaviour was in long-term decline. But with Islam on the rise, and many Christians—even those with the vaguest of personal beliefs—becoming more defensive of their cultural heritage, the line is getting harder and harder to draw.[1]

While many Europeans are proud of their secular traditions, many European countries have historical ties between religion and national identity, including England. The *Economist* explains:

England has an established church whose authority has been intertwined with the state's for five centuries. The powers of the Church of England have been trimmed and privileges have been granted to other religions. Yet although a mere 1.7 m[illion] people attend its services regularly, its special status endures. The queen is its head; Parliament approves its prayer book; and only last year did the prime minister relinquish the right to select its bishops, 25 of whom sit in the House of Lords.[2]

Writing in the British newspaper the *Guardian*, Elaine Glaser argued, "[I]f Britain really wants to integrate all its religious minorities, it must first separate church and state." She uses her experiences as a Jew at Christmas time to illustrate her point.

▲ Regent Street in London at Christmas

On my way to buy a sandwich at lunchtime, a 10-minute round trip at most, I pass seven Christmas trees, a poster advertising carol services, bountiful lamp-post decorations and an estate agent with computer screens forlornly garlanded with tinsel.

My attentiveness to these details is heightened by the fact that I am Jewish and, although not religious, celebrate Hanukah rather than Christmas with my family. Hanukah this year was on December 4 (it shifts with the lunar calendar), and perhaps due to its earliness it was even more invisible than normal. When I lurched back into work that afternoon with huge shopping bags and wrapping paper, my colleagues complimented me on my forward planning.

[There is a] . . . growing number of people who complain about politically correct schools banning nativity plays and other Christmas traditions. Why should non-Christians object, [he wondered]; after all, "can one imagine settling in a Muslim country and kicking up a fuss over it celebrating the end of

Ramadan?" I doubt he would enjoy hulking a fake Christmas tree home through the uncomprehending streets of Tehran or Islamabad. My yuletide resentment is a sign that Britain is not properly integrating its religious minorities. One fundamental reason for this failure is our refusal to consider the separation of church and state.

I often hear the argument that . . . Britain is only symbolically Christian. But Anglicanism is embedded in our political, legal and educational institutions—and, where identity and belonging are concerned, symbols are all-important.[3]

A similar debate has been waged over the language in the proposed constitution for the European Union. Some religious leaders—including Pope John Paul II and Pope Benedict XVI—have urged that the constitution should include a specific reference to Europe's Christian heritage; others warn that a reference to Christianity might be divisive but still believe there should be a reference to God. Still others maintain that the constitution should be entirely secular, with no religious references at all.

Connections

1. Should nations make some accommodation for different religious and cultural traditions in law? What might be gained? What are the dangers? How do you explain why accommodations have been made for some groups and not others?

2. Some argue that integration requires people to give up freedom of religion in order to fit in. For example, there have been debates across the world about the limits of religious expression. Are there times when it's appropriate to limit freedom of religion? What arguments might you make in favor of such proposals? What arguments might

be made against them? To what extent is it possible to make those decisions in a way that does not favor one religious tradition over others?

3. What does it mean for a country to be secular? How should secular nations accommodate religious differences? Consider the ways that Elizabeth Glaser says that she experiences Britain's Christian culture in her daily life. Are they violations of secularity? Do you think it's possible to create a truly secular society?

4. What are the official (government-sponsored) ways that religion influences life in your community? What are the unofficial ways that religion influences life in your community?

5. What does Glaser mean when she writes, "Where identity and belonging are concerned, symbols are all-important"? What symbols are important to her in this case?

6. What religious symbols do you see around your community? To what extent do they influence your sense of belonging? Do they contribute to your feelings of membership or make you feel more separate?

7. In July 2008, a Moroccan woman who wore a burqa—a full-body Islamic covering—was denied French citizenship because of "insufficient integration" into France. According to the ruling, "She has adopted a radical practice of her religion, incompatible with essential values of the French community." According to the French newspaper *Le Monde*, it was the first time a person's religious practice had been used to rule on his or her ability to be integrated in France.[4] To what extent should religious practice be used when considering a person's application for citizenship?

◇ ◇ ◇

[1] "Defining the limits of exceptionalism," the *Economist*, February 14, 2008, *http://www.economist.com/world/international/displaystory.cfm?story_id=10696111* (accessed March 17, 2008).

[2] "Sever them," the *Economist*, February 14, 2008, *http://www.economist.com/opinion/displaystory.cfm?story_id=10689643* (accessed March 17, 2008).

[3] Elaine Glaser, "Anglican amendment," the *Guardian*, December 19, 2007, *http://www.guardian.co.uk/christmas2007/story/0,,2229490,00.html* (accessed January 20, 2008).

[4] Angelique Chrisafis, "France rejects Muslim woman over radical practice of Islam," the *Guardian*, July 12, 2008, *http://www.guardian.co.uk/world/2008/jul/12/france.islam* (accessed July 15, 2008).

Believing in Britain

"The colour-blind humanity of most of my teachers, strength in the face of tyranny, taught us lessons for the rest of our lives."

E d Husain, author of *The Islamist*, grew up in a middle class immigrant family in London. In his memoir, he traces his path from primary school in the multicultural East End to his years in college as a religious extremist. After renouncing extremism, Husain moved to the Middle East, where, to his surprise, he felt stronger ties to British society than ever before. Horrified by the July 7, 2005, terrorist attacks in London, Husain returned home to warn others about the dangers of religious extremism. In this passage from his memoir, Husain remembers two key experiences from his childhood and speculates on how those experiences shaped his decisions.

▲ A British Bengali teenager in Whitechapel, East London

This reading contains excerpts from Ed Husain's, *The Islamist.*

Growing up in Britain in the 1980s was not easy. Looking back, I think [my teacher] Ms Powlesland was trying to create her own little world of goodwill and kindness for the children in her care. We grew up oblivious of the fact that large numbers of us were somehow different—we were 'Asian.' The warmth of the English fishermen in Upnor did not exist in the streets of east London.

'Pakis! Pakis! F— off back home!' the hoodlums would shout. The National Front [a nationalist party] was at its peak in the 1980s. I can still see a gang of shaven-headed tattooed thugs standing tall above us, hurling abuse as we walked to the local library to return our books. Ms Powlesland and the other teachers raced to us, held our hands firmly, and roared at the hate-filled bigots.

'Go away! Leave us alone,' they would bellow to taunts of 'Paki lovers' from the thugs. Little did I know then that one day, I, too, would be filled with abhorrence of others.

The colour-blind humanity of most of my teachers, strength in the face of tyranny, taught us lessons for the rest of our lives. Britain was our home, we were children of this soil, and no amount of intimidation would change that—we belonged here. And yet, lurking in the background were forces that were preparing to seize the hearts and minds of Britain's Muslim children.

I was the eldest of four, with a younger brother and twin sisters. My father was born in British India, my mother in East Pakistan [now Bangladesh], and we children in Mile End. My father arrived in England as a young man in 1961 and spent his early days as a restaurateur in Chertsey, Surrey. In ethnic terms I consider myself Indian. . . . Somewhere in my family line there is also Arab ancestry; some say from Yemen and others the Hijaz, a mountainous tract of land along the Red Sea coast in Arabia. This mixed heritage of being British by birth, Asian by descent, and Muslim by conviction was set to tear me apart later in life.

I remember my father used to buy us fresh cakes from a Jewish baker in Brick Lane. Our Koran school building had inherited mezuzahs on the door panels, which our Muslim teachers forbade us from removing out of respect for Judaism. My birthday, a family event at our home, is on Christmas Day. My mother would take us to see Santa Claus every year after [the] school Christmas party. We made a snowman in our garden, lending it my mother's scarf. Opposite our childhood home in Limehouse, a three-storey Victorian terrace, stood Our Lady Immaculate Catholic Church with a convent attached. We were friends of the sisters; our car was parked beside the nunnery every night. We helped out in the church's annual jumble sale. There was never any question of religious tension, no animosity between people of differing faiths. My mother still speaks fondly of her own childhood friends, many of whom were Hindu. But as I grew older, all that changed. The live-and-let-live world of my childhood was snatched away. . . .

It was a school rule that each term we were divided into dining groups of six; we lunched together and laid the table on a rota system. One day I forgot that it was my turn to help set the cutlery. Mr Coppin, mustachioed and blue-eyed, came into the dining hall and grabbed me by the arm. Taking me aside, he lowered his face to mine and yelled, 'Why didn't you set the table?'

'I forgot, Mr Coppin,' I whimpered.

'Forgot? How dare you forget?' he shouted, his hands resting on his knees. 'You're in trouble, young man! Do you understand?'

'Yes, Mr Coppin,' I said.

Then he said something that I have never forgotten. Of me, a nine-year-old, he asked, 'Where is your Allah now then, eh? Where is he? Can't he help you?'

What was he talking about? I wondered. What did Allah have to do with it? Besides, I did not even know precisely who Allah was. I knew Allah was something to do with Islam, but then I also wondered if Islam and Aslan from *The Lion, the Witch, and the Wardrobe* were in any way linked. After Mr Coppin's outburst, I thought it wiser not to ask.

Months before I left Sir William Burrough I had an accident on the school playground. I fell off a bike and cut my chin. Immediately Cherie, a teacher in whose classroom proudly hung a photo of her standing beside a waxwork of Margaret Thatcher at Madame Tussauds, rushed to help me. She drove me to hospital and held my hand throughout the entire ordeal of stitches and aftercare. As we stepped out of the hospital building she asked me if I wanted a piggy back. Thinking it was some sort of boiled sweet, I happily agreed.

Then, to my bewilderment, she went down on all fours and told me to climb on. I still remember her straightening her dungaree straps, and pushing back her glasses before taking off with me, an eleven-year-old Asian boy with a huge plaster on his chin, clinging on for dear life. Cherie drove me home and showered me with love and care in the days that followed.

That experience with Cherie, a white, non-Muslim teacher, and the commitment of Ms Powlesland and her staff to me and other pupils at Sir William Burrough stayed in my mind. It helped me form a belief in Britain, an unspoken appreciation of its values of fairness and equality. It would take me more than a decade to understand what drove Ms Powlesland and Cherie. I was fortunate to have such marvelous teachers at a young age. For later in life, when I doubted my affinity with Britain, those memories came rushing back.[1]

Connections

Identity Chart

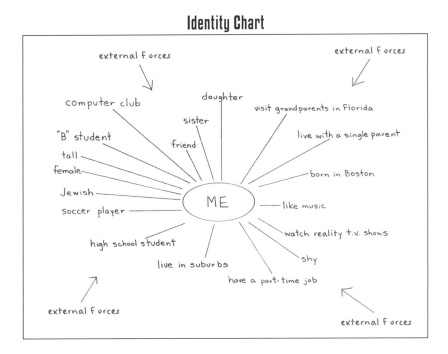

1. Using this model, create two identity charts for this reading, one before Husain is taunted by his teacher and one after he is saved by the other teacher. What did he learn from those experiences? How did those experiences shape his identity?

2. Have you had an experience at school that shapes how you see yourself and your relationship to the larger community? What was it?

3. What can we learn about integration from stories like those Husain shares in *The Islamist?*

4. Human Rights activist Arn Chorn Pond emigrated to the United States as a refugee and survivor of the Cambodian Genocide. He was brought to a rural school, where he struggled to fit in. His experiences transformed his community. A copy of a short film about Pond's experiences called *Everyone Has a Story* is available from Facing History and Ourselves. A reading about his story is also available at *www.choosingtoparticipate.org.*

◇ ◇ ◇

Reprinted from *The Islamist* by Ed Husain, Penguin Books, 2007. Copyright © Ed Husain, 2007.

---

[1] Ed Husain, *The Islamist: Why I Joined Radical Islam in Britain, What I Saw Inside and Why I Left* (London: Penguin Books, 2007), 1–5.

Changing Communities

"'We've been trying to get a place of worship for 30 years,' said Sheraz Arshard, 31, the Muslim leader here. . . . It's fitting it is a church: it is visually symbolic, the coming together of religions.'"

Newcomers bring with them ideas, customs, and traditions that may be unfamiliar to their host communities. One of the most visible of these institutions is a house of worship, where many immigrants congregate to retain their sense of identity and pass on their culture to the next generation. Some longtime residents argue that such changes break down the sense of community. Riem Spielhaus, an expert on Islam in Europe at Berlin's Humboldt University, explains that building mosques in Europe has become controversial because houses of worship have a powerful symbolic value. She explains, "The creation of a new mosque symbolically retraces the changes that have been made in society." New houses of worship are public reminders that newcomers intend to stay.

Sheraz Arshad at the former Mount Zion Methodist Church, which will become a mosque. Mr. Arshad fought for years to get Clitheroe to allow a place for Muslims to worship. ▶

Hazel Thompson for the *New York Times*

This reading contains excerpts from Jane Perlez's, "Old Church Becomes Mosque in Uneasy Britain," the *New York Times*.

Historically, religious congregations have often moved into buildings that once housed worshippers of another faith, but this now seems to be an increasingly common occurrence—and it is taking place in communities where it has not happened before.* One town experiencing such a transition is Clitheroe, England:

On a chilly night this winter, this pristine town in some of Britain's most untouched countryside voted to allow a former Christian church to become a mosque.

The narrow vote by the municipal authorities marked the end of a bitter struggle by the tiny Muslim population to establish a place of worship, one that will put a mosque in an imposing stone Methodist church that had been used as a factory since its congregation dwindled away 40 years ago.

The battle underscored Britain's unease with its Muslim minority . . . whose devotion has challenged an increasingly secular Britain's sense of itself.

Britain may continue to regard itself as a Christian nation. But practicing Muslims are likely to outnumber church-attending Christians in several decades, according to a recent survey by Christian Research, a group that specializes in documenting the status of Christianity in Britain.

. . . In Clitheroe, the tussle involved a passionate young professional of Pakistani descent coming up against the raw nerves of tradition-bound local residents.

---

* This is not a new phenomenon. For example, the cathedral of Cordoba, Spain, was a medieval mosque until the Catholic reconquest of Spain. In some cities of the United States, buildings built as synagogues for Jewish immigrants in the early 1900s have been converted to Christian churches.

"We've been trying to get a place of worship for 30 years," said Sheraz Arshad, 31, the Muslim leader here, his voice rattling around the empty old Mount Zion Methodist Church that will house his mosque. "It's fitting it is a church: it is visually symbolic, the coming together of religions." With a population of 14,500, a Norman castle and an Anglican church established in 1122, Clitheroe is tucked away in Lancashire County in the north. People here liked to think they represented a last barrier to the mosques that had become features in surrounding industrial towns. But Clitheroe had not bargained on the determination of Mr. Arshad, a project manager at British Aerospace. He is the British-born son of Mohamed Arshad, who came to Clitheroe from Rawalpindi [in Pakistan] in 1965 to work at the cement works on the town's outskirts.

When his father died in 2000, leaving his efforts to establish a mosque for the approximately 300 Muslims unfulfilled, Mr. Arshad took up the challenge.

"I thought, why should I be treated any less well?" Mr. Arshad said. "One quarter of my salary goes in tax, too. I was driven to do the mosque."

In all, Mr. Arshad and his father made eight applications for a mosque . . .

Often there was booing at council meetings, and, he said, cries of "Go home, Paki!"

The authorities' official reasoning for the rejections was generally that a mosque would attract outsiders—a veiled reference to Muslims—to Clitheroe.

. . . Mr. Arshad decided to get organized and demonstrate that he was a moderate Muslim who could take part in all the town's affairs.

He formed an interfaith scout group—Beaver Scouts—that honored many religious occasions, including the Taoist and Jewish new years. He established the Medina Islamic Education Center as an interfaith group for adults, and persuaded the local council to allow the group to lead a key committee. He organized a series of lectures on global conflict that attracted important academics.

On Dec. 21, the night of the vote on the mosque, the council chambers overflowed with 150 people. The police were poised outside. The vote was 7 to 5 for the mosque; there was no violence.

"I went in resigned to the fact we would lose," Mr. Arshad said. "In the end, it was very humbling."

"The church's [listing] as a place of worship in the town's planning records helped carry the day," said Geoffrey Jackson, chief executive of Trinity Partnership, a social welfare agency, and a Methodist who backed Mr. Arshad.

So did Mr. Arshad's demeanor. "He's a top lad, with a Lancashire accent, born and bred here, and educated at Clitheroe Grammar," Mr. Jackson said.[1]

Connections

1. What role do religious institutions play in the life of a community? Why do you think religion plays an important role in immigrant communities? How do those answers explain why it was important for Arshad to build a local mosque?

2. A positive outcome to the mosque building conflict presented in this reading is that it provides an opportunity to discuss issues not publicly addressed otherwise. What issues do you think these conflicts raise? How can these conflicts be turned into opportunities to promote integration?

3. How do you explain the initial resistance to Arshad's proposal at the town council meetings? What role did fear play? How did Arshad overcome that resistance?

◇ ◇ ◇

1 Jane Perlez, "Old Church Becomes Mosque in Uneasy Britain," the *New York Times*, April 2, 2007, *http://www.nytimes.com/2007/04/02/world/europe/02britain.html?pagewanted=print* (accessed November 8, 2007).

Accommodating Diversity

"My wife and I teach our children that different people do different things, behave in different ways, eat different foods, speak different languages, have different complexions, but that these differences amount to nothing more complicated, and nothing less spectacular, than the difference between flowers, each a different color, size, scent, and so on."

Cultural psychologist Carola Suárez-Orozco writes:

> Increasing globalization has stimulated an unprecedented flow of immigrants worldwide. These newcomers—from many national origins and a wide range of cultural, religious, linguistic, racial, and ethnic backgrounds—challenge a nation's sense of unity. Globalization threatens both the identities of the original residents of the areas in which newcomers settle and those of the immigrants and their children.[1]

For many people in host societies, their first exposure to the changes that come with migration is through the foods immigrants bring with them. Indian curries are now generally accepted as one of Britain's national dishes. Street food in Berlin now includes Turkish donner kebabs along with other, more traditional German treats. Tourists in Amsterdam and Paris seek out restaurants from former Dutch and French colonies. Couscous (a North African stew) is becoming as Parisian as steak frites (steak with french fries). Not everybody is happy about those changes; some people are worried that their culture is being lost. In fact, anti-immigrant groups in France are using traditional French food as a symbol of their message.

> Right wing [charity] groups in France have for weeks been handing out pork soup to the hungry. But dietary concerns

This reading contains excerpts from *Spiegel Online International*.

▲ Volunteers gather during a free pork soup distribution to homeless people near the Gare de l'Est railway station in Paris, France. Critics and some officials have denounced the charity distribution as discriminatory because the soup contains pork, which is off-limits to most Muslims and Jews.

mean that Muslims and Jews are excluded [because their religious dietary laws forbid the eating of pork]. Which is exactly the point. . . .

Those offering up the [pork soup] . . . deny that their charity is in any way racist or discriminatory. Pork soup, they say, is firmly rooted in traditional French cuisine and . . . they wouldn't refuse service to hungry Muslims or Jews.

"With pork in the soup, we return to our origins, our identity," Roger Bonnivard, head of homeless-support group Solidarity of the French and pork soup chef, told the Associated Press. "On every farm, you kill a pig and make a soup. . . . The pig is the food of our ancestors."

Others, however, have made it clear that there is a message behind the charity. "It's not that we don't like the Muslims," Bloc Identitaire [a right wing nationalist French group] leader

Frabrice Robert told the AP. ". . . Just 1,000 Muslims in France poses no problem, but 6 million poses a big problem."

In response to the soup kitchens, Strasbourg's Mayor Fabienne Keller declared that "[s]chemes with racial subtexts must be denounced." In his town, the so-called charity work of soup distributions was banned earlier this month. The police in Paris are considering similar actions.[2]

Claire Bonnivard, one of the soup kitchen organizers, explains that with increasing diversity, "our freedom in France is being threatened. . . . If we prefer European civilization and Christian culture, that's our choice."[3]

Shawkat Toorawa is a Muslim who writes about his identity. As a child he went to school in Paris. He remembers that the school cafeteria was one place where the differences between him and his classmates were visible. (His family ate only meat slaughtered according to Islamic dietary rules, called halal.) His parents emphasized that those differences were not something that had to be seen as negative:

At school, I was the only person who wouldn't eat meat in my age group. I would be given plain yogurt with two lumps of sugar and fruit when everyone else had meat. No one made fun of me, but I did ask my mother why I couldn't eat the meat my classmates were eating. We could, we just don't, she told me. We follow certain rules, others follow different rules. We aren't better than your friends, they aren't better than us. This sank in right away. My wife and I teach our children that different people do different things, behave in different ways, eat different foods, speak different languages, have different complexions, but that these differences amount to nothing more complicated, and nothing less spectacular, than the difference between flowers, each a different color, size, scent, and so on.[4]

In an effort to accommodate a growing Muslim population, a school in England has decided to serve only meat that has been slaughtered according to halal. While some parents support the changes, a number of opposing parents demonstrated in opposition. A mother of a student at the school explained her position:

> "I sent my kids to this school because I don't want them to be affected by religion. . . . We can't force our culture on someone else because that's not right so we shouldn't have someone else's culture forced on us. . . . The little culture that we have is being lost. . . . " She added: "I totally deny being guilty of racism. We allow people to come into this country and we end up being in a minority. We accommodate other cultures at the expense of ours."[5]

Connections

1. In the afterward to this book, Suárez-Oroszco writes, "The cultural challenges of identity formation in a global era affect immigrants and native born youth in different ways." How does immigration affect the identities of natives?

2. The Bloc Identitaire is a right-wing nativist group that uses messages of racial pride to "rally . . . young French and Europeans who are proud of their roots and of their heritage." How do you explain the appeal of nativist groups? Where is the line between being proud of your heritage and being intolerant of others?

3. Why do you think French officials kept Bloc Identitaire from distributing its soup? Do you agree with their decision? What did it accomplish? How else could the officials have responded?

4. What did Toorawa's family teach him about the differences between people? What do you think of the advice they gave him?

5. How did the administrators in the English school try to accommodate diversity? What do you think of the school's decision to serve halal-only meat in the cafeteria?

6. How does the English mother explain her decision to protest the cafeteria's policy? If you were a school official, what might you say to her? How might you try to resolve the conflict?

◇ ◇ ◇

Reprinted by permission from *Spiegel Online International* (January 25, 2008).

---

[1] Carola Suárez-Orozco, "Formulating Identity in a Globalized World," 173.

[2] "France Battling Bigot Broth for the Homeless," *Spiegel Online International*, January 25, 2006, *http://www.spiegel.de/international/0,1518,397249,00.html* (accessed September 19, 2007).

[3] Craig S. Smith, "In France, a meal of intolerance," *International Herald Tribune*, February 28, 2006, *http://www.iht.com/articles/2006/02/27/news/journal.php* (accessed November 6, 2007).

[4] Shawkat M. Toorawa, "Reflections of a Multicultural Muslim," (lecture, Northeastern University, Boston, MA, April, 19, 2001), available at *http://www.violence.neu.edu/Shawkat.Toorawa.html* (accessed October 7, 2008).

[5] "Parents protest at school's 'Halal-only' lunch," *Daily Mail*, February 9, 2007, *http://www.dailymail.co.uk/pages/live/articles/news/news.html?in_article_id=435198&in_page_id=1770* (accessed October 6, 2007).

Alienation

"You find yourself with people, you do not know their culture; you feel very bad, feel still more that you are not well integrated. . . ."

A crucial part of adolescence is a search for identity. For many adolescents, the pressures both from within and outside of their community present tough choices. Religion is an important and often positive component of a developing identity that can provide a framework of values, a sense of belonging, and direction to many adolescents as they navigate their environment. For some young Muslim adolescents in Europe, coming to terms with what it means to be in a religious minority is particularly difficult because they often do not feel accepted by society. In an interview, Souad, a French Maghrebin (North African) woman, describes how the divisions in French society were reflected in her classroom when she was a child:

> At middle and high school people sort themselves by group, as Maghrebins or as French. I felt that I shared more with Maghrebins than I did with the French. Already in the *sixième* [11 years old] we felt the difference between those whose parents had money and the others. They put me in the advanced section because I had received a 20 [an unusually high grade] in math the previous year; they thought they perhaps had an intellectual. It traumatized me that they put me with the others [French]. There was one girl who said: "You, you're Arab, don't get close to me." I was the "Arab of the classroom." It was really a shock. I was the only one, and I found it very hard to make friends; I made one. You find yourself with people, you do not know their culture; you feel very bad, feel still more

This reading contains excerpts from John Bowen's, *Why the French Don't Like Headscarves: Islam, the State, and Public Space* and Abd Samad Moussaoui's, *Zacarias, My Brother: The Making of a Terrorist.*

that you are not well integrated: "we don't want anything to do with you, you are Arab, dirty." They were taught this from their parents, the racism.

So the following year (*cinquième*) I came down to the ordinary level and was with people like me, of Maghrebin origin, and it was easier to get along, without the racism. And I really feel that the school system contributes to that because it is they who make the difference from the beginning, with only . . . French people at one level and all the Maghrebins and others in the other already in middle school, so it's normal that later on the racism will [have] grown in people's minds. So the schools have a responsibility.[1]

▲ North African immigrant boys playing on a rusted vehicle in France

© David Turnley/Corbis

What happens to young people who feel their identities are rejected by the larger society? Psychiatrist James Gilligan, author of *Preventing Violence: Prospects for Tomorrow*, warns that feelings of shame and humiliation are a key factor in understanding violence. He explains, "I have yet to see a serious act of violence that was not provoked by the experience of feeling shamed and humiliated, disrespected and ridiculed, and that did not represent the attempt to prevent or undo this 'loss of face'—no matter how severe the punishment, even if it includes death."[1]

Abd Samad Moussaoui, a French Muslim of North African descent, and his brother Zacarias both felt the sting of discrimination when they grew up in France. In his memoir, Abd describes how racism shaped the way they saw themselves and others:

> At La Fontaine, one of the teachers had a visceral hatred for North Africans. Incredible as it might seem, he did not hide his attitude. When he came across a student of Arab origins in the bathrooms, he would hit him. All the students knew that this went on, but nobody said anything. Zacarias got hit, I got hit, and so did others. In silence. It was *omertà*.* As if it only had to do with the teacher and us. As if this was the rule of a game laid on us by a racist teacher. Our goal was to keep one step ahead of him, never to be in the bathrooms when he was there.

> In such situations, a child does not really understand what's happening to him. He doesn't know why people are nasty. . . . When the child grows up, he learns how not to let it get to him. He learns to use his fists. And when he can lash out, he lashes out.[3]

---

* *Omertà* is secrecy sworn to by oath, a code of silence, or a refusal to give evidence to the police about criminal activities.

As they grew up, Abd and his brother responded to the discrimination they faced in different ways. Zacarias began to turn against those who he felt had rejected him, while Abd struggled to find his way in French society and eventually became a teacher. Zacarias fell under the influence of radicals who, in the name of religion, preached hatred, violence, and terrorism. While never excusing his brother's actions or ideology, Abd has tried to understand the path that led Zacarias to radicalism.

Connections

1. Souad felt alienated at school. She explains, "You find yourself with people, you do not know their culture; you feel very bad, feel still more that you are not well integrated. . . ." Why do you think that being the only North African in her class made her feel uncomfortable? Have there been times when you felt alienated from a larger group? How did it feel? What did you do about it?

2. What differences between students matter at your school? To whom do those differences matter? In the reading "The 'In' Group" from *Facing History and Ourselves: Holocaust and Human Behavior,* Eve Shalen writes:

   Usually, people are made outcasts because they are in some way different from the larger group. But in my class, large differences did not exist. It was as if the outcasts were invented by the group out of a need for them. Differences between us did not cause hatred; hatred caused differences between us.[4]

   How do you think Souad would respond to Shalen's comments? Do Shalen's comments describe how students perceive each other at your school?

3. Souad believes that "the school system contributes to [racism] because it is they who make the difference from the beginning, with only . . . French people at one level and all the Maghrebins [North Africans] and others in the other. . . . So the schools have a responsibility." In what ways do divisions in schools reflect larger social tensions? Do you believe that schools have a responsibility to mend those divisions? What can administrators and teachers realistically do?

4. A recent British government report on issues of identity and belonging at school explains:

> Meaningful contact between people from different groups has been shown to break down stereotypes and prejudice. Contact is meaningful when: conversations go beyond surface friendliness; . . . people exchange personal information or talk about each other's differences and identities; people share a common goal or share an interest; and they are sustained long-term.[5]

What would constitute meaningful contact between students from different groups? Does this happen at your school? If so, how and where? What are the educational benefits of "meaningful contact between people from different groups"? How could Souad's school have created opportunities for her and her classmates to have "meaningful contact"?

5. According to Moussaoui, how does being a victim of discrimination shape the way these people see themselves and others?

6. Give some examples of how people can respond to prejudice and discrimination. Why are some children resilient in the face of prejudice and discrimination while others are not?

7. In a paper commissioned by the British government on the radicalization of young Muslims, Tufyal Choudhury explains:

> One model identifying the 'attitudes' of individuals most at risk of radicalisation, identifies four 'essential' indicators: first, the

individual's perception of acceptance of them by society; second, their perceptions of equal opportunities; third, their sense of feeling integrated and part of society; and fourth, the extent to which they feel they identify with what they see as the dominant values of society. The extent to which society sees Muslims as part of the community is also important. All of these indicators are affected by mixed and contradictory messages from government and politicians.[2]

How do his comments relate to Moussaoui's attempt to understand his brother's choices? How do his comments echo Gilligan's about the relationship between humiliation and violence? What other factors should people consider when they try to understand why people commit violent acts?

8. Choudhury identifies several factors relating to identity and belonging that play a role in radicalization. Why do you think people embrace violent ideologies? What can be done to prevent young people from embracing violence when they feel excluded?

◇ ◇ ◇

[1] John R. Bowen, *Why the French Don't Like Headscarves: Islam, the State, and Public Space* (Princeton: Princeton University Press), 75.

[2] James Gilligan, *Violence: Reflections on a National Epidemic* (New York: Vintage Books, 1996), 110.

[3] Abd Samad Moussaoui, *Zacarias. My Brother: The Making of a Terrorist*, trans. by Simon Pleasance and Fronza Woods (New York: Seven Stories Press, 2003), 62-3.

[4] Eve Shalen, "The 'In' Group," *Facing History and Ourselves: Holocaust and Human Behavior* (Brookline: Facing History and Ourselves National Foundation, Inc., 1994), 29.

[5] Communities and Local Government, "Guidance on the duty to promote community cohesion," *http://www.culturaldiversity.org.uk/docs/38.pdf* (accessed January 25, 2008).

Identity and Belonging
in a Globalized World

◇ ◇ ◇

Talking About Religion

"My struggle to understand the traditions I belong to as mutually enriching rather than mutually exclusive is the story of a generation of young people standing at the crossroads of inheritance and discovery, trying to look both ways at once."

Too often, violence committed by extremists overshadows the stories of young people who are committed to building bridges between people of different religious traditions. Eboo Patel is the founder and executive director of the Interfaith Youth Core. The goal of the program is to create a community of young people who are working to foster understanding between people of different religious backgrounds. In his memoir, *Acts of Faith*, Patel describes the roots of his own activism:

> I am an American Muslim from India. My adolescence was a series of rejections, one after another, of the various dimensions of my heritage, in the belief that America, India, and Islam could not coexist within the same being. If I wanted to be one, I could not be the others. My struggle to understand the traditions I belong to as mutually enriching rather than mutually exclusive is the story of a generation of young people standing at the crossroads of inheritance and discovery, trying to look both ways at once. There is a strong connection between finding a sense of inner coherence and developing a commitment to pluralism. And that has everything to do with who meets you at the crossroads.
>
> When I was in college, I had the sudden realization that all of my heroes were people of deep faith: Dorothy Day, the Dalai Lama, Martin Luther King Jr., Mahatma Gandhi, Malcolm X, the Aga Khan. Moreover, they were all of different faiths. A little more research revealed two additional insights. First,

This reading contains excerpts from Eboo Patel's, *Acts of Faith: The Story of an American Muslim, the Struggle for the Soul of a Generation.*

religious cooperation had been central to the work of most of these faith heroes. The Reverend Martin Luther King Jr. partnered with Rabbi Abraham Joshua Heschel in the struggle for civil rights. Mahatma Gandhi stated that Hindu Muslim unity was just as important to him as a free India. Second, each of my faith heroes assumed an important leadership role at a young age. King was only twenty-six years old when he led the Montgomery bus boycott. Gandhi was even younger when he started his movement against unjust laws in early-twentieth-century South Africa.

. . . In high school, the group I ate lunch with included a Cuban Jew, a Nigerian Evangelical, and an Indian Hindu. We were all devout to a degree, but we almost never talked about our religions with one another. Often somebody would announce at the table that he couldn't eat a certain kind of food, or any food at all, for a period of time. We all knew religion hovered behind this, but nobody ever offered any explanation deeper than "my mom said," and nobody ever asked for one.

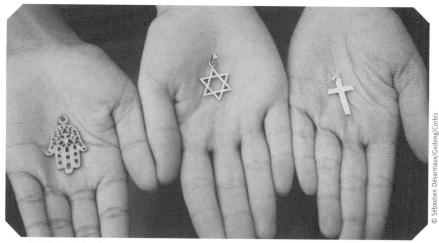

© Sébastien Désarmaux/Godong/Corbis

▲ Symbols of the three monothestic religions: Islam, Judaism, and Christianity

This silent pact relieved all of us. We were not equipped with a language that allowed us to explain our faith to others or to ask about anyone else's. Back then, I thought little about the dangers lurking within this absence.

A few years after we graduated, my Jewish friend reminded me of a dark time during our adolescence. There were a group of kids in our high school who, for several weeks, took up scrawling anti-Semitic slurs on classroom desks and making obscene statements about Jews in the hallways. I did not confront them. I did not comfort my Jewish friend. I knew little about what Judaism meant to him, less about the emotional effects of anti-Semitism, and next to nothing about how to stop religious bigotry. So I averted my eyes and avoided my friend, because I couldn't stand to face him.

A few years later, he described to me the fear he had experienced coming to school those days, and his utter loneliness as he had watched his close friends simply stand by. Hearing him recount his suffering and my complicity is the single most humiliating experience of my life. I did not know it in high school, but my silence was betrayal: betrayal of Islam, which calls upon Muslims to be courageous and compassionate in the face of injustice; betrayal of America, a nation that relies on its citizens to hold up the bridges of pluralism when others try to destroy them; betrayal of India, a country that has too often seen blood flow in its cities and villages when extremists target minorities and others fail to protect them.

My friend needed more than my silent presence at the lunch table. Pluralism is not a default position, an autopilot mode. Pluralism is an intentional commitment that is imprinted through action. It requires deliberate engagement with difference, outspoken loyalty to others, and proactive protection in the breach. You have to choose to step off the faith line onto the side of pluralism, and then you have to make your voice heard. To follow Robert Frost, it is easy to see the death of pluralism in the fire of a suicide bombing. But the ice of silence will kill it just as well.[1]

Connections

1. How did Patel overcome "rejection"? Who inspired him? What different traditions do they represent? What do they have in common? Who inspires you?

2. Patel believes that there is a connection between "inner coherence"— comfort with one's identity—and a commitment to pluralism—the peaceful coexistence of different groups. What does he mean? How can people balance their own identities and beliefs with a commitment to pluralism?

3. Religion is an important part of Patel's identity. Does religion play a role in the way you see yourself and others?

4. Reflecting on his silence, Patel explains that his friends were not equipped to discuss their faith with other people or to ask questions about the differences between their traditions. How can young people become prepared to talk about these issues? What does Patel mean when he talks about the "dangers lurking within this absence"?

5. Patel says that he and his friends were bystanders while Jews were intimidated at school. Have you ever been a bystander? Describe the situation. Why didn't you get involved? How do you and your friends respond when people of different groups feel intimidated by racism and prejudice? How would you like to respond?

6. Who is responsible for responding to racist or antisemitic incidents at school? The teachers? The students? The parents?

◇ ◇ ◇

---

[1] Eboo Patel, *Acts of Faith: The Story of an American Muslim, the Struggle for the Soul of a Generation* (Boston: Beacon Press), xvii–xix.

A New Concept of Identity

"If . . . people cannot live their multiple belongings, if they constantly have to choose between one side or the other, if they are ordered to get back to their tribe, we have the right to be worried about the basic way the world functions."

A min Maalouf, a French writer and author of the book *In the Name of Identity: Violence and the Need to Belong*, lives in France. He believes that at the root of much of the world's violence are tensions about identity and belonging. To prevent violence, Maalouf writes that we need to find a new way to think about identity:

▲ How can you imagine new forms of identity?

© Sébastien Désarmaux/Godong/Corbis

In the age of globalization and of the ever-accelerating intermingling of elements in which we are all caught up, a new concept of identity is needed, and needed urgently. We cannot be satisfied with forcing billions of bewildered human beings to choose between excessive assertion of their identity and the loss of their identity altogether, between fundamentalism and disintegration.[1]

Maalouf illustrates his point by sharing some of his own story:

Since I left Lebanon in 1976 to establish myself in France, I have been asked many times, with the best intentions in the

This reading contains excerpts from Amin Maalouf's, *In the Name of Identity: Violence and the Need to Belong*.

world, if I felt more French or more Lebanese. I always give the same answer: "Both." Not in an attempt to be fair or balanced but because if I gave another answer I would be lying. This is why I am myself and not another, at the edge of two countries, two or three languages and several cultural traditions. This is precisely what determines my identity. Would I be more authentic if I cut off a part of myself?

To those who ask, I explain with patience that I was born in Lebanon, lived there until the age of 27, that Arabic is my first language and I discovered Dickens, Dumas and "Gulliver's Travels" in the Arabic translation, and I felt happy for the first time as a child in my village in the mountains, the village of my ancestors where I heard some of the stories that would help me later write my novels. How could I forget all of this? How could I untie myself from it? But on another side, I have lived on the French soil for 22 years, I drink its water and wine, my hands caress its old stones everyday, I write my books in French and France could never again be a foreign country.

Half French and half Lebanese, then? Not at all! The identity cannot be compartmentalized; it cannot be split in halves or thirds, nor have any clearly defined set of boundaries. I do not have several identities, I only have one, made of all the elements that have shaped its unique proportions.

Sometimes, when I have finished explaining in detail why I fully claim all of my elements, someone comes up to me and whispers in a friendly way: "You were right to say all this, but deep inside of yourself, what do you really feel you are?"

This question made me smile for a long time. Today, it no longer does. It reveals to me a dangerous and common attitude men have. When I am asked who I am "deep inside of myself," it means there is, deep inside each one of us, one "belonging" that matters, our profound truth, in a way, our "essence" that is determined once and for all at our birth and never changes. As for the rest, all of the rest—the path of a free man, the beliefs he acquires, his preferences, his own sensitivity, his affinities, his life—all these things do not count. And when we push our contemporaries to state their identity, which we do very often these days, we are asking them to search deep inside of themselves for this so-called fundamental belonging, that is often religious, nationalistic, racial or ethnic and to boast it, even to a point of provocation.

Whoever claims a more complex identity becomes marginalized. A young man born in France of Algerian parents is obviously part of two cultures and should be able to assume both. I said both to be clear, but the components of his personality are numerous. The language, the beliefs, the lifestyle, the relation with the family, the artistic and culinary taste, the influences—French, European, Occidental—blend in him with other influences—Arabic, Berber, African, Muslim. This could be an enriching and fertile experience if the young man feels free to live it fully, if he is encouraged to take upon himself his diversity; on the other side, his route can be traumatic if each time he claims he is French, some look at him as a traitor or a renegade, and also if each time he emphasizes his links with Algeria, its history, its culture, he feels a lack of understanding, mistrust or hostility.

The situation is even more delicate on the other side of the Rhine. Thinking about a Turk born almost 30 years ago near Frankfurt, and who has always lived in Germany, and who speaks and writes the German language better than the language of his Fathers. To his adopted society, he is not German, to his society of birth, he is no longer really Turkish. Common sense dictates that he could claim to belong to both cultures. But nothing in the law or in the mentality of either allows him to assume in harmony his combined identity.

I mentioned the two first examples that come to my mind. I could have mentioned many others. The case of a person born in Belgrade from a Serb mother and a Croatian father. Or a Hutu woman married to a Tutsi. Or an American that has a black father and a Jewish mother.

Some people could think these examples unique. To be honest, I don't think so. These few cases are not the only ones to have a complex identity. Multiple opposed "belongings" meet in each man and push him to deal with heartbreaking choices. For some, this is simply obvious at first sight; for others, one must look more closely.

If . . . people cannot live their multiple belongings, if they constantly have to choose between one side or the other, if they are ordered to get back to their tribe, we have the right to be worried about the basic way the world functions.

"Have to choose," "ordered to get back," I was saying. By whom? Not only by fanatics and xenophobes of all sides, but by you and me, each one of us. Precisely, because these habits of thinking are deeply rooted in all of us, because of this narrow, exclusive, bigoted, simplified conception that reduces the whole identity to a single belonging declared with rage.

I feel like screaming aloud: This is how you "manufacture" slaughterers![2]

According to Maalouf, stereotypes matter whether they come from within the group or outside of it. Reducing people's identity to narrow categories, he explains, can lead to violence.

Connections

1. Maalouf believes that globalization is putting new pressures on people to claim an identity. How? Why does he think people are forced to "choose between excessive assertion of their identity and the loss of their identity altogether, between fundamentalism and disintegration"? Where does this pressure come from?

2. This reading is called "Deadly Identities." Why does Maalouf think that identities can be dangerous?

3. Maalouf asserts that "identity cannot be compartmentalized; it cannot be split in halves or thirds, nor have any clearly defined set of boundaries. I do not have several identities, I only have one, made of all the elements that have shaped its unique proportions." What does he mean? How do you think about the many parts that make up your own identity?

4. Does your identity, or the way you express it, change in different situations? How does the way you define yourself differ from the way society might define your identity?

5. Identify a moment when an aspect of your identity was affirmed. How did this make you feel? How did you respond? Identify a moment when an aspect of your identity was rejected or demeaned in some way. How did this make you feel? How did you respond?

6. In *Facing History and Ourselves: Holocaust and Human Behavior*, there is a children's story called "The Bear That Wasn't" about a bear that is made to believe that he is a lazy man wearing a fur coat who should be working in a factory. Throughout the story he is told by many different people that he is not who is thinks he is. How does this parable illustrate the tensions Maalouf describes?

◇ ◇ ◇

Reprinted by permission from *Al Jadid Magazine* (www.aljadid.com), Fall 1998.

---

[1] Amin Maalouf, *In the Name of Identity: Violence and the Need to Belong* (New York: Arcade Publishing, Inc., 2001), 35.

[2] Amin Maalouf, *Les identités meurtriè* [Deadly Identities] (Grasset, 1998), trans. by Brigitte Caland, *Al Jadid* Vol. 4, No. 25 (Fall 1998), *http://leb.net/~aljadid/essays/DeadlyIdentities.html* (accessed July 12, 2007).

More Than a Headscarf

". . . You identify with that one factor within you that stands out. But in another country, like in a Muslim country, . . . if someone asked us to identify ourselves, we would say we were American. It's what you don't take for granted, I guess, that identifies you in that location."

Muslims, like other religious minorities, often struggle to find a balance between conforming to society and retaining their distinct cultural identity. Increasingly, Muslim women in Europe and the United States have begun to wear the hijab—or headscarf—as a matter of pride, a statement of identity, and a sign of religious commitment. In the United States and elsewhere, the wearing of the hijab has raised questions about whether these women see themselves first as Muslims or Americans.

▲ Muslim and Jewish students attend a reception at the Middle East Coexistence House on the Douglass College campus at Rutgers University in New Brunswick, New Jersey.

This reading contains excerpts from Judy Woodruff's, "Young Muslims Struggle with Identity," National Public Radio.

National Public Radio correspondent Judy Woodruff spoke to two sisters, Assia and Iman Boundaoui, about growing up as children of Algerian immigrants in Bridgeview, Illinois. Their conversations raised difficult questions about the headscarf, stereotypes, and the role of religion in the national identity of the United States.

Woodruff's story included an interview with a group of friends who described what it's like for them to grow up as Muslims in the United States:

Assia BOUNDAOUI: . . . Just 'cause you wear a [head]scarf people think that you are an immigrant . . . You know, I'm proud to be Algerian, but it makes me mad when people think just because you have a scarf on, you can't be American. You know, they have to ask you where are you really from? No, no, where are you really from?

Iman BOUNDAOUI: When we went to 4th of July—4th of July we go to this park where they do fireworks and there's entertainment and whatever. We go there usually, like, every year. And I felt like—we all felt completely normal, but then Assia kind of felt like don't you feel like people are staring at us. Like, this is like all-American, you know, holiday and here we are with, like, scarves and do we feel out of place. And I'm, like, no. You know what I mean? . . .

WOODRUFF: . . . When it comes to your own identity, do you think of yourself first as Muslim or American?

A. BOUNDAOUI: Okay, in America, we would say we're Muslim first. Right? Because that's what makes us different I guess. So you identify with that one factor within you that stands out. But in another country, like in a Muslim country, and if someone asked us to identify ourselves, we would say we were American. It's what you don't take for granted, I guess, that identifies you in that location. You know what I mean? . . .

WOODRUFF: As I sat down to talk with them in the family living room, I realized this was an opportunity to pose some basic questions that strangers, non-Muslims, are curious about but rarely have the chance to ask. How many scarves do you have?

I. BOUNDAOUI: Oh my God! We have like a hundred!

A. BOUNDAOUI: But it's like asking, how many blouses do you have? You know what I mean? . . .

WOODRUFF: Women may wear the hijab so people don't judge them by their appearance, but by wearing it some people do judge them precisely by their appearance.

Inevitably, the scarf advertises that they're Muslim. The Boundaoui sisters say after 9/11 a few women in their neighborhood removed their headscarves out of fear. Others who hadn't worn them before decided to put them on out of pride.

A. BOUNDAOUI: That's a question everyone asks you. Is life different after 9/11? But I think, in my mind, what's changed is when people maybe didn't see me before, they see me now very clearly. Now that they see me, they sort of have to decide how they feel about me, you know?

WOODRUFF: What do you mean by that? What do they say when they see you out in public? What do they see?

A. BOUNDAOUI: Sometimes it's hostile, and sometimes they're curious.

WOODRUFF: Iman, what do you think?

I. BOUNDAOUI: Well, other people, I felt like they saw somebody who was oppressed. And some people would just say, you know, you're in America now. You can take it off. You don't have to be wearing it.

A. BOUNDAOUI: Yeah. No offense, but why do you wear a scarf? I think the pervasive misconception is that Muslim women are held down by hijab; it's a tool that men use to oppress them. But that's such an alien idea to us, because it's really such a personal choice.

You know, the United States is this free country, and people choose—women that choose to wear scarves in America are especially conscious of their freedom. So a Muslim woman's choice to wear it in America is especially poignant, I guess.

WOODRUFF: You're saying it's a choice.

A. BOUNDAOUI: Right.

WOODRUFF: You've grown up in a Muslim family where you were expected as young women to wear it.

A. BOUNDAOUI: Mm-hmm. Right.

I. BOUNDAOUI: Everyone expects it, but there was no forceful action. I thank God my mom was never that type to say, you know, it's time now; you have to put it on. My mom left it up to us.

WOODRUFF: How old were you when you started wearing it?

I. BOUNDAOUI: I was 15. . . .

WOODRUFF: You know, you are being asked because of your religion to grapple with and confront some very difficult decisions at a younger age that so—in a way, so many other people your age don't have to think about.

A. BOUNDAOUI: I think it makes us stronger. It's hard in the beginning, because we feel that we have to prove ourselves I guess. Like over the past year I was working at a law firm. I was there for a year and I was the only Muslim and I was wearing a scarf, you know. And I felt like, wow, the pressure is on. All these people have these preconceived ideas of who you are, and you have to show them otherwise that, you know, I'm more than my scarf. I am a political science major. I am interested in this. I do that. You know, I am more than a scarf . . .

WOODRUFF: Twenty-year-old Assia Boundaoui and her 18-year-old sister Iman. Assia talked about struggling with wearing the hijab, and several weeks after this interview she told us she's decided, at least for now, to stop wearing it.

In an e-mail to us she writes: Hijab will always be a spiritual force within me. It isn't a mere external covering; it is modesty manifested in every aspect of my life, in my actions, words and choices. I've chosen not to embody hijab physically, but it remains an integral force in my life. My decision has been completely supported by my family.[1]

Connections

1. How do you explain the increasing popularity of the hijab among young Muslim women? What role does the hijab play in the Boundaoui sisters' identity? What other words might you use to describe them?

2. Sometimes the sisters see themselves as more American, and other times they feel more Muslim. How do you explain their perceptions? Are there times when you feel that your own identity shifts and you feel more or less of one identity? Why do you think you might feel that way?

3. In discussing young Muslim women who are choosing to wear the hijab, Mubarak, former president of the Muslim Students Association, explained that, "these kids are comfortable in their American identity because that's the only culture they've known, so it's easier for them to embrace the outward manifestations of Islam." What does she mean? Why would comfort with their American identity make it easier for young women to wear the hijab?

4. How do the Boundaoui sisters challenge traditional assumptions about what it means to be an American? Why do you think the image of young Americans wearing hijabs makes some people uncomfortable?

5. How do people in your school use fashion to project their identity? What is the difference between wearing the hijab as a statement of identity and wearing other clothes or symbols to represent who you are?

6. What values do people associate with the hijab? Give examples of the assumptions some people make about others because of the clothes they wear.

This reading is based on a National Public Radio interview. Follow this link to listen to the entire interview: *http://www.npr.org/templates/story/story.php?storyId=6071738.*

◇ ◇ ◇

Reprinted by permission from National Public Radio (September 14, 2006).

1 Judy Woodruff, "Young Muslims Struggle with Identity," National Public Radio, September 14, 2006, *http://www.npr.org/templates/story/story.php?storyId=6071738* (accessed September 20, 2006).

What Does Integration Look Like?

"The controversies over public declarations of Islamic identity are perhaps the best sign that the new generation of European Muslims is no longer immigrants, but vocal and engaged Europeans."

Shortly after the end of World War II, many European countries turned to their colonies in the developing nations and recruited hundreds of thousands of laborers from rural areas. The majority of these immigrants came from Muslim majority countries, although for decades these immigrants, like many others, attempted to get by and blend in, and Islam was not an overt part of their daily lives. It is estimated that after War World II, there were roughly one million Muslims living in Europe. These "guest workers" came to aid in the postwar reconstruction efforts, and they were expected to return home when their work

▲ A Turkish woman writes the word *Integration* on a blackboard in a classroom in Hamburg-Wilhelmsburg, Germany.

© Patrick Lux/DPA/epa/Corbis

Portions of this reading were written by Carla Power exclusively for *Stories of Identity.*

was done. But over time it became clear that they were in Europe to stay. By the 1970s many of these "guests" became immigrants and, in a decade or two, fellow citizens. Despite the oil crisis of 1973, a recession, and the legal attempts to stop the immigration into Europe that followed, family unification programs and a persistent demand for cheap labor kept the inflow of immigrants steady.

Muslims make up the majority of these immigrants, and while there are no official numbers, demographers estimate that between 15 and 20 million Muslims live in Europe. They represent roughly 5 percent of the total population. With the increased visibility of Muslims in Europe, some commentators have argued that they are developing into a parallel society—one that does not blend in with the whole. Yet, in large and small ways, integration is occurring. The question explored in this reading is, "What does integration look like?"

By now, it's a passion play of 21st century Europe. A Muslim girl or woman insists on wearing a headscarf, or the fully enveloping niqab in public—at school or court or as a doctor in a hospital operating theater, say—and European civilization declares itself under attack. Whether it's the furors over French Muslim schoolgirls' insistence of wearing headscarves to school, or the British battles over the rights of women teachers and judges to cover their faces with the niqab, these debates are nearly always cast as signs of cultural schisms between Islam and the West. Conservatives fret about European values being under attack by the advancing hordes from the Muslim East, while liberals worry about women's human rights being undermined by religious duties. For many, the hijab battles are signs that European Muslims aren't yet fully European, and that integration is failing.

In fact, it's anything but. The controversies over public declarations of Islamic identity are perhaps the best sign that the new generation of European Muslims is no longer immigrants, but vocal and engaged Europeans. The veil's new ubiquity—on city streets and in European courthouses and classrooms—is a sign of integration, albeit veiled integration. When British member of Parliament Jack Straw complained that it was hard to interact properly with the women who came to his office wearing niqabs, many Britons agreed. The democratic process was undermined, suggested the British press, by the women who were effectively faceless. Few noticed that they were there to see their member of parliament, exercising their rights as tax-paying citizens to engage in dialogue with their elected representative, something their migrant mothers and grandmothers probably never would have known to do, or dared.

When Muslim migrants began arriving in Britain and France in the 60s and 70s, they kept their heads down, concentrating on working factory shifts and driving cabs and saving for the day they'd return "home." Their children and grandchildren, by contrast, are European-born and educated, with a sense of entitlement to the democratic process, to religious freedom, to equality in the workspace and at school. "This is a new generation that makes fewer concessions," observes Mohammed Colin, editor of the French Muslim news-site SaphirNews. "My mother believed in absolute assimilation. But me, I haven't got anything to prove. I'm French, and France is multicultural."

It's not to say that moving from the margins to the mainstream is painless. Striking the middle course between embracing life in Europe and Muslim values is a challenge perhaps at least as great as being an isolated migrant. "The challenge of Islam," observes Asim Siddiqui, a British Muslim accountant, "is not to socially withdraw from the world. That's too easy. The challenge is to engage with the world, to see where it takes you, and to have as much engagement as possible." As Muslims slowly break their way out of migrant ghettos and into the mainstream European middle class, there are new tensions. In Britain, one of the main stumbling blocks for ambitious young Muslims is the pub: if drinks after work are key for getting ahead, what is the Muslim account manager to do if he wants a promotion? For the Muslim in France, where the Republic's cherished principle of *laicism** means that public life is zealously protected from religion, a woman who wants to work and wear a veil will most likely find herself confined to the back office, or if she's less lucky, simply jobless and back home.

The greatest challenge for French Muslims, observes Colin, is "visibility." But visibility is a sign of engagement. Europe's new Muslim visibility—whether veiled women, or minarets thrusting up in city skylines, or Muslim political pressure groups—is a sign, paradoxically, of how very European its Muslims have become.[1]

Connections

1. Carla Power writes, "The controversies over public declarations of Islamic identity are perhaps the best sign that the new generation of European Muslims is no longer immigrants, but vocal and engaged Europeans." What does she mean? What examples does she use to make her point?

2. Mohammed Colin, editor of the French Muslim news-site SaphirNews, explains, "This is a new generation that makes fewer concessions. My mother believed in absolute assimilation. But me, I haven't got anything to prove. I'm French, and France is multicultural." How do you explain the difference between these two generations?

---

* *Laicism* or *laïcité*, is French for secularity. The term comes from the word *lay* or *laity*, which refers to Christians who did not belong to religious orders or to the clergy.

3. Colin explains that the greatest challenge for French Muslims is "visibility." How do immigrants become visible? What are some of the challenges that come with visibility? What are some of the opportunities?

◇ ◇ ◇

Used by permission of Carla Power (September 16, 2008).

---

[1] Carla Power, "Muslim Integration," (working paper, September 16, 2008).

Afterword

Transnational Identities in Our Globalized Societies

By Carola Suárez-Orozco, Professor of Applied Psychology,
Co-Director of Immigration Studies, New York University

"The healthiest path is one in which transcultural youth creatively fuse aspects of two or more cultures—the parental tradition and the new culture or cultures. In so doing, they synthesize an identity that does not require them to choose between cultures—but rather allows them to develop an identity that incorporates traits of both cultures, all the while fusing additive elements."

In our increasingly globalized societies, people from an array of cultural, religious, linguistic, racial, and ethnic backgrounds share the same work, educational, and living spaces in new ways rarely encountered before in the same scale. This reality presents challenges to newcomers who settle in a new land, to their children and grandchildren, as well as to the original residents of the areas in which they settle. Integrating immigrants and the subsequent generations into the receiving society is clearly a primary challenge of globalization, and to fail to do so will have long-term social implications. True integration requires transculturative identity work on both sides of the equation—the "newcomers" as well as the longer-term residents. For newcomers, an ability to formulate an identity that allows fluid transcultural movement between the family-of-origin's world and the new land is a primary task of adaptation and well-being. For those growing up in diverse spaces, the most adaptive approach is to develop a "cosmopolitan" identity that embraces a sense of belonging to a global culture of inclusion.[1]

"Newcomers," the Social Mirror, & Forging Transcultural Identities

For first-generation immigrants who arrive as adults, identity is deeply rooted in their birthplace. While many expatriates are quite comfortable in their new homeland, they nonetheless tend to retain an outsider status, as their cultural and linguistic hurdles are simply too high to be surmounted within one generation.[2] The path for their children—the second generation—is less straightforward, offering a variety of paths to be taken. For these youth, forging a sense of identity is a significant developmental challenge. Do they feel comfortable in their homeland? Do they feel accepted by the "native-born" of the host country? What relationship do they have with their parents' country of origin? Is their sense of identity rooted "here," "there," everywhere, or nowhere?

In forming an identity, youth attempt to create a self-identity that is consistent with how others view them. Identity is less challenging when there is continuity between the various social milieus youth encounter—home, school, neighborhood, and country. In the era of globalization, however, social spaces are more discontinuous and fractured than ever before. The tension between the dominant culture and minority newcomers is at the heart of the ethnic and cultural identity-formation drama of immigrants and their children. Youth are challenged to navigate between achieved identities and ascribed or imposed identities.[3] The achieved identity is the extent to which an individual achieves a sense of belonging—"I am a member of this group." An ascribed identity is imposed either by co-ethnics—"You are a member of our group"—or by members of the dominant culture—"You are a member of that group." The work of identity formation is to synthesize the two.

The general social climate, or ethos, of reception plays a critical role in allowing young people to forge a sense of belonging and adapt to their new land.[4] Unfortunately, intolerance for newcomers is an all too common response all over the world. Discrimination against immigrants of color is particularly widespread and intense in many areas receiving large numbers of new immigrants—be it in the United States, in Japan, or all over Europe. As today's immigrants are more diverse than ever before in ethnicity, skin color, and religion, they are particularly subject to the pervasive social traumata of prejudice and social exclusion.[5]

These exclusions can take a structural form (when individuals are excluded from the opportunity structure) as well as an "attitudinal" form in the form of disparagement and public hostility, or what I term the "social mirror."[6] These structural barriers and the social ethos of intolerance and racism encountered by many immigrants of color intensify the stresses of immigration. Although the structural exclusion suffered by immigrants and their children is tangibly detrimental to their ability to participate in the opportunity structure, the attitudinal social exclusion also plays equally a toxic role. Philosopher Charles Taylor argued that "our identity is partly shaped by recognition or its absence, often by the misrecognition of others, and so a person or group of people can suffer real damage, real distortion, if the people or society around them mirror back to them a confining or demeaning or contemptible picture of themselves."[7] How can youth of immigrant origin incorporate the notion that they are unwanted "aliens" who do not warrant the most basic rights of education, health care, or recognition?

We are all highly dependent upon the reflection of ourselves mirrored by others.[8] When the image reflected back to us is generally positive, we are able to feel that we are worthwhile and competent. When the reflections are consistently of sloth, irresponsibility, low intelligence, and danger and these images are received in a number of mirrors including the media, the classroom, and the street, it is nearly impossible to maintain an untarnished sense of self.[9]

How do youth respond to the negative social mirror? One possible pathway is for youth to become resigned to the negative reflections, leading to hopelessness and self-depreciation that may in turn result in low aspirations and self-defeating behaviors. In this scenario, the child is likely to respond with self-doubt and shame, setting low aspirations in a kind of self-fulfilling prophecy: "They are probably right. I'll never be able to do anything." Other youth may mobilize to resist the mirrors and injustices they encounter. Without hope, the resulting anger and compensatory self-aggrandizement may lead to acting-out behaviors that look like: "If you think I'm bad, let me show you just how bad I can be."[10]

The social and educational trajectories of youth are more promising for those who are able to actively maintain and cultivate a sense of hope for the future. Those who are able to maintain hope are in fundamental ways partially inoculated to the toxicity they may encounter. These youth are better able to maintain pride and preserve their self-esteem, mobilize their coping resources, and respond to the negative social mirror with: "I'll show you I can make it in spite of what you think of me."[11]

Without hope, some youth of immigrant origin . . . may develop an adversarial stance, constructing identities around rejecting—after having been rejected by—the institutions of the dominant culture. Among youth engaged in adversarial styles, speaking the standard language of the host culture and doing well in school may be viewed by their peers as a form of ethnic betrayal; under such circumstances it may become problematic for them to develop the behavioral and attitudinal repertoire necessary for academic success.

The children of immigrants who are not able to embrace their own culture and who have formulated their identities around rejecting aspects of the mainstream society in some contexts may be drawn to gangs. For such youth, gang membership, in the absence of meaningful opportunities, becomes incorporated into their sense of identity. Gangs offer their members a sense of belonging, solidarity, protection, support, discipline, and warmth. Gangs also structure the anger many feel toward the society that violently rejected their parents and themselves. Although many second-generation youth may look towards gangs for cues about dress, language, and attitude, most remain on the periphery and eventually outgrow the gang mystique after working through the identity issues of adolescence. Others . . . drawn to the periphery—and to the epicenter of gangs—are disproportionally represented in the penal system. The gang ethos provides a sense of identity and cohesion for marginal youth during a turbulent stage of their development while they are also facing urban poverty and limited economic opportunity, ethnic minority status and discrimination, lack of training and education, and a breakdown in the social institutions of school and family.[12]

While many adversarial youth may limit their enactment of delinquent behaviors within their neighborhoods, for others an adversarial stance may lead to extreme nationalism or radicalism. There is a very small proportion of disenfranchised second-generation youth who become enraged at the consistent misrepresentation, misunderstanding, and misperception about their ethnic, religious, or country of origin group. Again, the social mirror plays a critical role in this radicalized stance. Algerian-born Kamel Daoudi, raised in France and arrested on suspicion of being part of an al Qaeda plot to blow up the American embassy in Paris, wrote: " . . . I became aware of the abominable social treatment given all those potential 'myselves' who have been conditioned to become subcitizens just good for paying pension for the real French. . . . There are only two choices left for me, either to sink into a deep depression, and I did for about six months . . . or to react by taking part in the universal struggle against the overwhelming unjust cynicism."[13] Today, throughout most of the Western world, Muslims are "designated Others" serving as the targets of reflexive hatred. As a result, daily representations in the news media depict the actions of a few with enormous repercussions on many. This in turn . . . feeds long-distance nationalism and extremist stances that have horrific implications for the youth themselves, their communities, and the societies that receive them.

Other youth may respond to the negative mirror by trying to shed their culture of origin altogether. Taking ethnic flight, these youth may feel most comfortable spending time with peers from the mainstream culture rather than with their less acculturated peers. For these youth, identifying with the dominant culture and success in school may be seen not only as a route for individualistic self-advancement, but also as a way to symbolically and psychologically move away from the world of the family and the ethnic group. In an earlier era, this style of adaptation was termed "passing." While there were gains for racial and ethnic minorities who "disappeared" into the mainstream culture, there were also costs—primarily in terms of unresolved shame, doubt, self-hatred, and loss of family and community. While "passing" may have been a common style of adaptation among those who phenotypically "locked" like the mainstream, it is not easily an option to today's immigrants of color who visibly look like the "other." Further, while ethnic flight is a form of adaptation that can be adaptive in terms of "making it" by the mainstream society's standards, its significant social and emotional toll is too great a burden.

Clearly, the healthiest path is one in which transcultural youth creatively fuse aspects of two or more cultures—the parental tradition and the new culture or cultures. In so doing, they synthesize an identity that does not require them to choose between cultures—but rather allows them to develop an identity that incorporates traits of both cultures, all the while fusing additive elements.[14] For Latinos, this state is what Ed Morales refers to as "living in Spanglish." He defines the root of Spanglish as "a very universal state of being. It is displacement from one place, home, to another place, home, in which one feels at home in both places, yet at home in neither place. . . . Spanglish is the state of belonging to at least two identities at the same time, and not being confused or hurt by it."[15] Such is the identity challenge of youth of immigrant origin—their developmental task requires crafting new cultural formations out of two systems that are at once their own and foreign. These children achieve bicultural and bilingual competencies that become an integral part of their sense of self.

For many young people, the choice is not between their own homogenous parental home culture, which is consistent with their neighborhood and nation's culture, and the cultural context which is receiving them (which would imply a bicultural identity). Rather the choices can be between a mother from one nation, a father from another, while residing in a diverse neighborhood and attending an equally diverse school while imbedded in a metropolitan city. In a case like this and the myriad variations repeated across the globe, the choice is much more of a transcultural identity. In the words of Henry Louis Gates, Jr., "Today the ideal of wholeness has largely been retired. And cultural multiplicity is no longer seen as the problem but as a solution—a solution that defines identity itself. Double consciousness, once a disorder, is now a cure. Indeed the only complaint we moderns have is that Du Bois was too cautious in his accounting. He'd conjured 'two souls, two thoughts, two unreconciled strivings.' Just two, Dr. Du Bois? Keep counting."[16]

Transcultural identities are most adaptive in this era of globalism and multiculturalism. By acquiring competencies that enable them to operate within more than one cultural space, immigrant youth are at an advantage. The key to a successful adaptation involves acquiring

competencies that are relevant to the global economy while maintaining the family relations, social networks, and connectedness essential to
well-being. Those who are at ease in multiple social and cultural contexts
will be most successful and will be able to achieve higher levels of matu-
rity and functioning.

Globalized Identity in the Receiving Society

Globalization is contributing significantly to a world that is increasingly
multicultural. There is much to celebrate in this process while recognizing
that diversification presents real challenges to both the individuals enter-
ing new spaces as well as those living in receiving spaces. The greatest
danger of diversification is an increase in intolerance and the accompa-
nying violence this may engender. Diversity, at the same time, should be
recognized as presenting a tremendous opportunity for individuals and
societies to search for unifying commonalities of human experience.

Is there such a thing as a global identity? In recent decades, American
youth culture has come to dominate the cultural scene among adolescents living in urban centers in Europe, Latin America, and Asia.[17] This
pattern seems in large part to be driven by the global media, including movies, television, music videos and recordings, global markets, and
the Internet. Developmental psychologist Jeffrey Jensen Arnett argues
that globalization has clear implications for identity development among
youth. He maintains that increasingly the majority of young people in
the world are developing "bicultural" identities that incorporate elements of their local culture along with awareness of their relation to the
global youth culture, presenting new challenges to identity formation
and development.[18]

The cultural challenges of identity formation in a global era affect immigrants and native-born youth in different ways.[19] For the children of immigrants the task is to braid together, into a flexible sense of self, elements
of the parent culture, the new culture they are navigating along with an
emerging globalized youth culture. For those in the host society, the
challenge is to broaden the cultural horizon to incorporate the changing
perspectives, habits, and potentials of its diverse newcomers.

Many struggle to manage the inconsistencies and ambivalences of multiple cultural menus.[20] On one hand the challenge may be particularly extreme when there is significant "cultural distance" between the country of origin and the host country.[21] For many children of immigrants, the diminished ties to any one cultural context "may result in an acute sense of alienation and impermanence as they grow up with a lack of cultural certainty, a lack of clear guidelines for how life is to be lived and how to interpret experience."[22] On the other hand, harnessing the innate optimism of youth while providing adequate cultural interpreters, educational opportunities, and a reasonably welcoming reception in the new culture allows youth to quickly become successful members of their society.

Developing a sense of belonging to a global culture has clear potential benefits.

> "Because the global culture crosses so many cultural and national boundaries, in order to unify people across these boundaries, the values of the global culture necessarily emphasize tolerating and even celebrating differences. This means that the values of the global culture are defined in part by what they are not: They are not dogmatic: they are not exclusionary, they do not condone suppression of people or groups who have a point of view or a way of life that is different from the majority."[23]

As educators, we have a responsibility to place the tolerance—and even celebration—of cultural differences at the very core of our educational agenda. Such an "end" could serve to provide a core meaningful educational narrative that "envisions a future . . . constructs ideals . . . prescribes rules of conduct, provides a source of authority, and above all gives a sense of continuity of purpose."[24] Tolerance must be fostered not only in those who already reside in the receiving context but also among the widely diverse newcomers who are sharing the new social space. Preparing our youth to successfully navigate in our multicultural world is essential to preparing them to be global citizens. As our world becomes increasingly intertwined, surely the need for greater tolerance and understanding is more obvious than ever before.

[1] Kwame Anthony Appiah, *Cosmopolitanism: Ethics in a World of Strangers* (New York: W. W. Norton Co., 2006); J. J. Arnett, "The psychology of globalization," *American Psychologist*, vol. 57 #10 (2002): 774–783.

[2] Carola Suárez-Orozco and Marcelo Suárez-Orozco, *Children of Immigration* (Cambridge: Harvard University Press, 2001).

[3] Ibid.

[4] Carola Suárez-Orozco, "Formulating Identity in a Globalized World," as quoted in *Globalization: Culture & Education in the New Millennium*, ed. Marcelo Suárez-Orozco and Desiree Baolin Qin-Hillard (Berkeley: University of California Press, 2004), 173–202; Carola Suárez-Orozco and Marcelo Suárez-Orozco, *Children of Immigration*; Carola Suárez-Orozco, Marcelo Suárez-Orozco, and Irina Todorova, *Learning a New Land: Immigrant Students in American Society* (Cambridge: Belknap Press of Harvard University Press, 2008).

[5] Beverly Daniel Tatum,*"Why Are All the Black Kids Sitting Together in the Cafeteria?" And Other Conversations About Race* (New York, Basic Books, 1997).

[6] Carola Suárez-Orozco, "Identities Under Siege: Immigration Stress and Social Mirroring Among the Children of Immigrants," as quoted in *Cultures Under Siege: Social Violence and Trauma*, ed. Marcelo Suárez-Orozco (Cambridge: Cambridge University Press, 2000): 194–226.

[7] Charles Taylor, *Multiculturalism: Examining the Politics of Recognition* (Princeton: Princeton University Press, 1994).

[8] D. W. Winnicott, *Playing and Reality* (Middlesex: Penguin, 1971); Carola Suárez-Crozco, "Identities Under Siege: Immigration Stress and Social Mirroring Among the Children of Immigrants."

[9] Carola Suárez-Orozco, "Identities Under Siege: Immigration Stress and Social Mirroring Among the Children of Immigrants."

[10] Ibid.

[11] Carola Suárez-Orozco and Marcelo Suárez-Orozco, *Children of Immigration*.

[12] James Diego Vigil, *Barrio Gangs: Street Life and Identity in Southern California* (Austin: University of Texas Press, 1988).

[13] Elaine Sciolino, "Portrait of the Arab as a Young Radical," the *New York Times*, September 22, 2002.

[14] C. J. Falicov, "The Family Migration Experience: Loss and Resilience," as quoted in *Latinos: Remaking America*, ed. Mariela Paez (Berkeley: University of California Press, 2002).

[15] Ed Morales, *Living in Spanglish: The Search for Latino Identity in America* (New York: St. Martin's Press, 2002): 6–7.

[16] Henry Louis Gates, Jr., "Both Sides Now," the *New York Times Book Review*, May 4, 2003, 31.

[17] Carola Suárez-Orozco and Marcelo Suárez-Orozco, *Children of Immigration*.

[18] J. J. Arnett, "The psychology of globalization."

[19] J. J. Arnett, "The psychology of globalization"; A. Bame Nsamenang, "Adolescence in Sub-Saharan Africa: An Image Constructed from Africa's Triple Inheritance," as quoted in *The World's Youth: Adolescence in Eight Regions of the Globe*, ed. T. S. Saraswathi (New York: Cambridge University Press, 2002), 61–104; Carola Suárez-Orozco, "Formulating Identity in a Globalized World."

[20] Nsamenang, "Adolescence in Sub-Saharan Africa: An Image Constructed from Africa's Triple Inheritance."

[21] James W. Berry, "Immigration, Acculturation, & Adaptation," *International Journal of Applied Psychology*, vol. 46 (January 1997), 5–34.

[22] J. J. Arnett, "The psychology of globalization," 778.

[23] Ibid., 779.

[24] Neil Postman, *The End of Education: Redefining the Value of School* (New York: Knopf, 1995).

Glossary

antisemitism: A certain perception of Jews, which may be expressed as hatred towards Jews. *Antisemitism* frequently charges Jews with conspiring to harm humanity, and it is often used to blame Jews for why things go wrong. It is expressed in speech, writing, visual forms and action and employs sinister stereotypes and negative character traits.

assimilation: A process through which immigrants accept the national culture of the host country and give up their former national identity.

community cohesion: A shared sense of belonging and purpose among members of a group who come from different backgrounds.

diaspora: A term that originates from the Greek word meaning "dispersion," *diaspora* refers to the community of people that migrated from their homeland. For example, the Jews who live outside of Israel are often called the "Jewish diaspora."

French Revolution (1789–1799): During this political and social upheaval, the "Third Estate" (the common people) overturned the French monarchy and established a revolutionary government based on the principles of popular sovereignty. France's revolutionary government took over vast properties owned by the church, the aristocracy, and the nobility and distributed them among the peasantry. With "liberty, equality, and fraternity" as its slogan, the *French Revolution* became an inspirational model for future democratic revolutions.

globalization: The increasing flow of people, ideas, commodities, languages, and traditions throughout the world. Modern transportation, migration, e-business, multinational companies, and trade agreements, as well as the use of the Internet and cell phones, speed up this process and contribute to a "global culture" that some fear threatens the diversity of human cultures.

hijab: Originating from the Arabic word for "curtain," it is a veil worn by many Muslim women in observance of their faith. Hijab is a means of preserving one's modesty, as well as a display of cultural affiliation and religious devotion. The *hijab* is one name for a variety of similar head-scarves that cover the head and neck, and often the hair and forehead.

interfaith: A term that describes actions, events, or organizations that bring together persons of different religious faiths and affiliations.

Islamist: Often described as fundamentalists, *Islamists* preach that Islam is not only a religion, but also a social and political system that governs most aspects of life. The majority of *Islamists* attempt to replace secular governance in a peaceful manner, but a small minority of them resorts to extreme measures, including violence and even terrorism.

mezuzah: A small, ornamental case containing scriptural text on parchment, found on doorposts to traditional Jewish homes; a *mezuzah* serves to remind Jews of their religious commitment.

Montgomery bus boycott: Led by Martin Luther King, Jr., in 1956, this year-long boycott of public transportation in Montgomery, Alabama, gained national attention for the civil rights movement. The *Montgomery bus boycott* protested the segregation of public transit systems in the United States.

nationalism: A political ideology that emphasizes national culture or interests above those of minorities and other sub-national groups.

nativist: One who believes that the interests of native-born citizens should be favored over those of immigrants.

parallel societies: A community in which members of different backgrounds lack a shared sense of group identity and thus live separately, side by side.

radicalism: A political orientation that favors extreme changes to society, sometimes by resorting to violence.

sharia: An Islamic term, literally "the path to the watering place," which implies the expression of Allah's command for Muslim society. Generally thought of as a legal code based on the Qur'an, the term today can refer to both religious laws and religiously inspired ethics.

Sufi: One who practices Sufism, a mystical Islamic tradition. Sufis believe that by letting go of all notions of identity and individuality, one can realize divine unity.

transcultural/transnational identity: *Transcultural* is a term that refers to how people act as members of different cultural or national communities. "Transcultural identity" is a source of individual identity that draws from across national boundaries and cultural, religious, linguistic, and ethnic backgrounds.

Volk: The term *Volk* (pronounced "folk") literally means "people." Volk implies that citizenship in the national community is inseparable from blood relations. Volk includes language, custom, history, and mythology shared by all German people. In the 1930s and 1940s, the term was used to justify the persecution of the Jews, who were deemed a threat to the purity of the German nation. Some proposed the word *Bevölkerung,* which means "population," to signify the diversity of German citizens.

Westernization: The process of adopting or imposing customs originating from North American and Western European countries.

xenophobia: Fear and hatred of foreigners or immigrants. It comes from the Greek words *xenos,* meaning "foreigner" or "stranger," and *phobos,* meaning "fear."